Revised and Updated

Cloud

WILD STALLION OF THE ROCKIES

Revised and Updated

Cloud

WILD STALLION OF THE ROCKIES

*A companion book
to the program seen
on public television's
NATURE series*

Ginger Kathrens

CompanionHouse
BOOKS

Cloud: Wild Stallion of the Rockies

CompanionHouse Books™ is an imprint of Fox Chapel Publishers International Ltd.

Project Team
Vice President–Content: Christopher Reggio
Editor: Amy Deputato
Copy Editor: Laura Taylor
Design: Mary Ann Kahn
Index: Elizabeth Walker

ISBN 978-1-62008-242-3

Library of Congress Cataloging-in-Publication Data
Names: Kathrens, Ginger, 1946- , author.
Title: Cloud, wild stallion of the Rockies / Ginger Kathrens.
Description: Mount Joy, PA : Fox Chapel Publishers International Ltd., 2017.
    | Includes bibliographical references and index. | Originally published:
    Irvine, California : BowTie Press, 2001.
Identifiers: LCCN 2017040708 (print) | LCCN 2017042421 (ebook) | ISBN
    9781620080504 (ebook) | ISBN 9781620082423 (softcover)
Subjects: LCSH: Cloud (Horse)--Juvenile literature. | Wild horses--Rocky
    Mountains Region--Biography--Juvenile literature. | Kathrens, Ginger,
    1946---Juvenile literature. | Human-animal relationships--Juvenile
    literature.
Classification: LCC SF360.3.R53 (ebook) | LCC SF360.3.R53 K38 2017 (print) |
    DDC 599.665/50978--dc23
LC record available at https://lccn.loc.gov/2017040708

This book has been published with the intent to provide accurate and authoritative information in regard to the subject matter within. While every precaution has been taken in the preparation of this book, the author and publisher expressly disclaim any responsibility for any errors, omissions, or adverse effects arising from the use or application of the information contained herein.

Fox Chapel Publishing
903 Square Street
Mount Joy, PA 17552

Fox Chapel Publishers International Ltd.
7 Danefield Road, Selsey (Chichester)
West Sussex PO20 9DA, U.K.

www.facebook.com/companionhousebooks

We are always looking for talented authors. To submit an idea, please send a brief inquiry to acquisitions@foxchapelpublishing.com.

Printed and bound in Singapore
20 19 18 17   2 4 6 8 10 9 7 5 3 1

Contents

Introduction

I shoot movies for a living. Not the kind of movies you see in the theatre, but films about what's going on in the wilderness. These are documentaries you're likely to see on television channels such as PBS.

Lugging film equipment over rugged mountains, through swamps and insect-ridden rain forests, is not what most people do for fun. And you'd think it wouldn't be fun for me, especially since my equipment weighs more than I do. But I love the challenge of finding out what lives on the other side of the mountain or on the far side of the swamp, and then quietly filming it. Nothing could be more exciting to me.

When Marty Stouffer, host and producer of the popular PBS series *Wild America*, asked me to film a documentary about wild horses in 1994, I jumped at the chance. At the same time, I was worried. Though I grew up on a farm in Ohio and had my own horse, I knew absolutely nothing about wild horses. So I set out to learn as much as I could.

On a trip with my sister to research potential shooting locations, I visited the remote Arrowhead Mountains of southern Montana and saw my first family of wild horses. This band was led by a magnificent black stallion who was named Raven. Years before, probably when he was a foal, he had been named by wild-horse admirers. Though he and the band, along with their newborn foal, ran away at the sight of us, I felt an unusual connection to them. I was hopeful that, in time, they might get used to me.

This would be a good location, I thought. The mountains, canyons, and deserts of the Arrowheads would make a photogenic backdrop for a film, and the mostly open country would allow me to spot the wild horses at a distance. I could try to get as close as possible to the horses on two rough four-wheel-drive roads that wind up the mountain ridges of the horse range. Then I could hike shorter distances with the heavy gear. I could use powerful camera lenses to bring the horses up close without interfering with their daily lives.

As I began filming my program, Raven, his three mares, and their foals and yearling son appeared time and again. Strange as it seems, I felt they were finding me rather than me finding them. Was their story destined to become the focus of mine? I learned how to make myself less threatening, watching to see which direction the band was going.

Then I positioned myself well ahead of them in plain sight. I sat very still. If they chose to come closer, I reasoned, it would be their decision. Amazingly, they grew accustomed to me hanging out with them. They allowed me to eavesdrop on their intriguing lives, and I fell in love with each and every one of them. I also fell into the magical spell of their homeland, which was once the spiritual center of the great Crow Indian Nation. It was as wild, mysterious, and spectacular as the horses themselves. The summer I spent in the Arrowhead Mountains was a wonderful, unforgettable experience.

In September, the Bureau of Land Management (BLM), which is in charge of managing wild horses on our public lands, had a roundup. Roundups are held to keep wild horse populations in balance with their environment. Animals who are removed are offered for sale. This roundup proved to be tragic for Raven's family. Two of the three foals died in what was a terrible trauma for them and a nightmare for me.

The following spring, nothing could keep me from returning to the Arrowheads to look for what remained of Raven's band. I had to learn if this wonderful family of horses could start anew and recapture what seemed to be a magical and joyous time. This is where our story begins.

Maps

MONTANA

⊗

WYOMING

Missoula

Great Falls

Fort Peck Lake

Missouri R.

HELENA   MONTANA

Billings

Gillette

WYOMING   Casper

Laramie   CHEYENNE

For two hundred years, wild horses have wandered this isolated corner of the Rocky Mountains, a flat-topped range that the Crow Indians called the Arrowhead Mountains.

ONE

A Family
of
Wild Horses

Raven lifted his head and looked out over the windswept ridges of his mountain home. For two hundred years, perhaps longer, wild horses have wandered this isolated corner of the Rocky Mountains, a flat-topped range that the Crow Indians called the Arrowhead Mountains. Two of the black stallion's mares grazed nearby as their filly foals slept on the sunny hillside. The only clue to the presence of the two little fillies was the occasional flick of a stubby tail appearing over tufts of windblown grass.

Raven's two fillies had been the first foals born on the mountain. On a crisp, sunny day in mid-March, I had spotted them through binoculars, a mile off, in the desert lowlands near the base of the mountain. Later, when I could see them closer, I named the chunky reddish-brown filly Mahogany and her more delicate sister Smokey. Both had stars on their foreheads like their father and their mothers.

The two fillies were inseparable. They explored around the juniper bushes in the lowlands, and investigated downed logs and mysterious little rock outcropping. They groomed each other, nibbling on those hard-to-reach places like just behind their wooly upright manes. Sometimes, they stood butt to butt and rubbed for all they were worth, creating a sort of rhythmic mustang mamba. Only when it came to meals did they split up to nurse.

The mothers of the newborns were as different as night and day. Mahogany's mother was a small, pale buckskin, a color the Native American people called claybank because it matched the nearby riverbanks. She seemed quiet and easygoing like her yearling son, who I had named Diamond. The other mare was larger and darker, a short-tempered horse I had named Grumpy. When the two fillies and Diamond kicked up their heels, running and jumping, Grumpy interceded like the "fun police." She signaled the youngsters to cool their jets with a simple ears-back, head-bent, don't-fool-with-me gesture. It seemed to work every time.

Raven shook his head, revealing a bright white star under a forelock so long it nearly reached the white snip on the end of his nose. The stallion was restless and alert.

Raven's chunky, reddish-brown filly Mahogany has a star on her forehead like her father and mother.

When the little fillies wandered too far from the band, it was Raven's job to bring them back. Lowering his head to the ground, he stretched out his neck in what is called *snaking*, and gently herded his errant daughters home. Mothers can't do this job because they run the risk of being stolen by marauding stallions looking for mares.

Raven shook his head, revealing a bright white star under a forelock so long it nearly reached the white snip on the end of his nose. The stallion was restless and alert. It is the job of the stallion father not only to guard his mares but also to protect his foals and yearlings. Together, stallion, mares, foals, and yearlings form a family group called a *band*. Raven knew at this moment that he was missing an important member of his family. It was late May and the height of foaling season.

Only hours before, I had watched Raven's youngest mare, a four-year-old palomino, disappear into a stand of dense Douglas fir trees. She was heavy with foal, so I guessed she might be going away to have her baby. Most wild foals are born under cover of darkness in a spot well hidden from their main predator, the mountain lion. Lions in the Arrowhead Mountains prey mainly on mule deer and newborn foals. I hoped the young mare would hide herself well.

*I watched the white colt intently.
In an instant, the name came to
me—I would call him Cloud.*

TWO

Cloud's Birth

I turned to see the palomino walking calmly from behind the firs. With her was a spindly colt who took my breath away.

I returned to the mountain the next morning. It was sunny and still, a warm day for late May in the high country of the Rockies. By mid-morning I had not yet found Raven and his family, but I was watching an immature three-year-old stallion with fascination. He was trying to breed his father's newly acquired red roan mare. Usually when young stallions reach the age of two, they are kicked out of their bands by their fathers. In this way, wild horses avoid inbreeding. This youngster had been allowed to stay with his family, although I thought his days were numbered.

Again and again the young mare tried to rebuff the advances of the young stallion, kicking him squarely in the chest with resounding thuds. Only when his father returned did the young male retreat, opening and closing his mouth apologetically like a tiny foal, as if to say, *Don't hurt me, I'm little.*

Then, out of the corner of my eye, I caught some movement and a flash of light color through the trees. I turned to see the palomino walking calmly from behind the firs. Following her was a spindly colt who took my breath away. The color of his coat was blindingly white. His sisters flashed past him at a trot. Then came the older mares, and then Diamond. The little foal tottered after his mother on long, rickety legs. Raven walked just behind them, acting as rear guard. The colt looked terribly thin, yet he appeared determined to keep up the brisk march. I knew where they were going. During spring, the mountaintop was still buried in deep snow while the water holes in the low country had dried up. The horses were going to find water in the only accessible place. They were going to the lingering drifts under the canopy of the Douglas firs more than halfway up the mountainside.

I followed the band at a cautious distance, wondering how far the fragile youngster could travel before keeling over in his tracks. But he kept going. To fall behind was unthinkable for the colt. The family group is central to the emotional well-being and survival of every member, especially a tottering newborn. The colt tried to keep his body touching his mother's as they climbed.

It must have been a mile or more before the band stopped at the first large snowbank in the deep shade of fir trees. The horses pawed the drifts and then ate huge bites of snow. Water dribbled out of the corners of their mouths. Exhausted, the white colt slumped near the trunk of a tree, laid his head down, and fell asleep. Pale purple pasque flowers poked their heads through the moist ground. They grew at the edges of the snowbank near where the colt lay. A mountain chickadee whistled a high-pitched mating call, and a pine squirrel chattered excitedly in the distance.

Did I hear a rustling in the forest, in some dark recess where the sun seldom shone? I stared into the darkness and imagined a mountain lion moving stealthily into position. The large cats wait quietly in the shadows to ambush an unsuspecting quarry. Once detected, they have little chance to make a kill. Ridiculous, I concluded. No mountain lion would creep this close to a human or to cautious adult horses. Still, I worried that this bright little colt might invite unwanted attention.

Through binoculars, I watched the white colt intently. I could see his ribs heave up and down and his fuzzy ears twitch at an occasional fly. The sun dipped behind a huge thunderhead, and I felt a chill breeze off the snowbanks. In that instant, the name came to me—Cloud, I would call him Cloud. And then I prayed he would live.

Raven's band was easily identified by his two light-colored mares. Now there was a third bright light in the family: little Cloud.

THREE

The White Colt

Two weeks later, wild horse family bands, twenty family groups in all, were following the green upward, working their way to the top of the mountain. And so was I. My four-wheeler lurched and groaned over rock slabs, ruts, and sandy gullies as I climbed the two-track road leading to the mountaintop and, I hoped, to Cloud.

The red desert disappeared in my rear-view mirror as I passed through the meadows where I'd first seen the white colt. Higher up, I slid around curves and through puddles in the dense Douglas fir forest. The snowbanks had nearly disappeared, giving way to clusters of pasque flowers. Their fuzzy blossoms soaked up sun shining in slits between dark trunks and the litter of deadfall.

The higher I drove, the more my excitement grew. I splattered through puddles a foot deep. Finally, near the top of the mountain, I broke out of the trees. Ahead lay the wide, rolling subalpine meadows and clusters of fir trees. Named long ago by the Crow Indians, these Arrowhead Mountains were the heart of their spectacular homeland.

Immediately in front of me, limestone cliffs rimmed a treeless, teacup-shaped bowl. Below the cliffs, a huge snowfield clung to the steep slope. Beneath the snowfield in the open meadow I saw a coyote loping along, dragging a long bone. I'd seen coyotes here before and

Duns (right) have a black line down their back, tiger stripes on their legs, and even stripes across their shoulders at times. Grullas (left) are gray with the same primitive markings.

was certain they must have a den nearby. As the coyote disappeared into the trees with his prize, I concluded with relief that the leg was way too big for a little foal. It was the back leg of an adult horse who maybe had died in the tough winter or during last fall's roundup. Every few years, the calm of the Arrowheads is shattered when the Bureau of Land Management rounds up horses to keep their population small, some say too small to guarantee a healthy horse herd for years to come. Injuries are always possible.

A sharp scream pulled me around. Only one animal makes this haunting call. It was the battle cry of a stallion. A band of three horses crested the hilltop and galloped down the sides of the bowl. In the rear was a golden dun stallion with a coal-black mane, tail, and legs. He was snaking his mare and yearling away from what—a predator or another stallion? The wise old dun had been named Shaman by some admiring human when he was a youngster a dozen years or more ago.

Suddenly the source of the danger revealed itself in the form of a sleek black horse, a bachelor stallion, intent on winning Shaman's mare. He thundered down the hill toward the small band. Shaman wheeled and rushed out, launching himself at the black, rearing and then spinning and kicking the younger horse squarely in the side. The two squealed in anger as they stood on their hind legs, flailing at the air and gnashing their teeth. Then, just as suddenly as the fight had begun, it was over. The black stallion trotted a short distance off. Shaman had won for now, but he knew the black stallion would be back, and he eyed him warily.

The mare and yearling started to graze. Even Shaman let down his guard and grazed alongside his family. The horses below me were typical of the Arrowheads, small in stature and dark or earth tone in color. Many, like Shaman, were duns with a black line down their back, tiger stripes on their legs, and even stripes across their shoulders at times. Others were gray with the same primitive markings. This is a color called *grulla*, Spanish for "crane-colored" or "mouse-colored." Duns and grullas are wonderfully camouflaged, making them difficult to see as they roam their wilderness home.

To the east of the bowl, the flat-topped Bighorn Mountains loomed, still buried in deep snow. Flashes of color caught my eye on a knoll in the foreground. Through my binoculars, a light buckskin, a palomino, and a small white foal were walking uphill. Cloud. It was

Cloud! He was alive and following his family to the top of the mountain. Raven was in the rear, protecting the family from any danger below, and the palomino was proudly in the lead with her white colt. They were followed by the buckskin mare and Mahogany, then the grulla mare, Grumpy, and Smokey, and finally the blue roan yearling, Diamond. They were making their first journey of the season to the high meadows.

Some family groups have signature animals who reveal the identity of their bands in an instant. That's the way it was with Raven's band with his two light-colored mares. And now there was a third bright light in the family, little Cloud.

My four-wheeler slipped and slid along the muddy two-track road atop the mountain as I drove as fast as I dared. I was fairly certain I knew where Raven and his family were headed. I knew of a beautiful water hole that is an early summer favorite of the horses. If my hunch was right, Raven's band would be there in only a few minutes. I leaped out of my four-wheeler and nearly ran across the meadow from the road. Quietly, I sat on a little rock outcropping that gave me a view of the sparkling water hole below.

The blue roan band stallion, Plenty Coups, was drinking with his grulla mare and three yearlings. Two of the yearlings, a dun and a blue roan, had been orphaned when their mothers were rounded up the previous fall. The elegant five-year-old stallion had added the foals to his little band. He was named Plenty Coups in honor of the last chief of the Crow Indians. So great and revered a leader was Chief Plenty Coups that the Crow decided never to have another. They knew they would never find a man to match his courage and wisdom. The great chief had no children of his own, so he adopted orphans, just as his young stallion namesake had done.

As Raven and his band appeared on the hill above the water hole and headed down to the water, Plenty Coups's head jerked up, and his mare and the three yearlings began to move off. Plenty Coups followed. In wild horse society, when a more powerful group moves in, the subordinate band will give ground.

The palomino trotted downhill. Cloud followed, dancing into a trot, no longer teetering on unsteady legs. He broke into a run, giving a little buck of excitement. A visit to the water hole must be as fun for the horses as going to the swimming pool is for kids. Cloud's sisters and brother raced down with their mothers. Raven plunged in and began to paw the water, churning it into muddy waves.

Little Cloud held back and watched as the mares drank, rolled, and pawed. He ventured close enough to dip his pink-snipped nose into the pond but jerked back, surprised by the cool wetness of it. Until now, he had tasted only his mother's milk and an occasional bite of slushy snow. But this was water. Slowly he waded in ankle-deep but backed quickly out to watch.

When Raven finished pawing, he left the water for a sandy spot and rolled. Over and over he rolled, encrusting his body in mud. Only his head was clean, his white star and snip still shining. Raven had learned from watching his parents that mud helps ward off biting insects and can dry-clean the coat. Cloud switched his attention from his father to Smokey, who flopped down and dusted herself in a protective shroud. When the mares began to trail off, the foals obediently but reluctantly followed. Raven took up the rear.

That evening, I walked onto the meadows and found the band grazing in the setting sun. I waved as I approached. I had learned it was nearly impossible to sneak up on wild horses. They may smell you and think you are a predator. Then they do what nature has taught them to do to survive. They run away. Announcing my presence with a wave gave them the opportunity to size up this two-legged intruder. It seemed to work well if I sat down some distance from the band. That way it was their choice to come closer to me if they wanted to.

Once the sun disappeared behind the hills, the clouds turned fiery red and the temperature dropped in a hurry. That's when Cloud and his sisters began to play, running and bucking, then putting on the brakes, only to burst off again. Cloud's favorite game was to race around a circular grove of firs. They were perfectly designed for running laps. His sisters soon tired of racing around the cluster of trees and began to

In a rare moment, Cloud stops his frolicking to engage in mutual grooming with his sister Mahogany.

nibble on each other's backs; a feel–good rubdown called *mutual grooming*. Not Cloud. He thought nothing was more fun than running. Around and around he circled at top speed. Then he suddenly quit and nickered for his mother, who nickered back. He walked over to nurse for a few minutes and collapsed on his side.

In the weeks that followed, I watched Cloud grow into a precocious colt who liked to pester his sisters. When they would lie down for a nap, he would stroll over and begin pulling on their manes and tails. If that didn't get a reaction, he would begin nibbling on their faces and pulling on their ears. Finally, they had to get up and play. Sometimes they would explore the dark places at the forest edges with their pesky little brother in the lead. Any noise, such as wind rustling the branches or a deer running away or ravens flying overhead, could send the three foals dashing back to their mothers.

Cloud seemed different from the other colts on the Arrowheads. He seemed more daring and outgoing, and more observant. Nothing within earshot or eyesight passed by him. When the sorrel band stallion, Flash, snaked his black mare and foal away from a group of bachelor stallions by laying his ears back and dropping his head nearly to the ground, Cloud watched. Then, when a little filly came near his band, Cloud imitated the band stallion, laying his ears flat to his head and lowering his head. He swaggered toward the filly, who got the message immediately and ran back to her mother. I felt sorry for her. She was the only foal in her band and had come to play on the day Cloud decided to demonstrate what a big, tough stallion he was.

Cloud watched his brother Diamond play-fight with a grulla yearling from another band. The two young stallions reared on their hind legs and pawed at each other, then bowed low and bit at each other's legs. The two whirled and bumped into each other. All their play was preparation for the time when play would turn serious, for the time they would battle to win a mare. But that was years away for these yearlings. Most stallions arc six before they are mature enough to try and steal a mare.

Cloud watched his brother intently. When Diamond tired of playing with the yearling and returned to his band, Cloud marched up and picked up where Diamond had left off. He reared up at the big yearling and bumped into him. The grulla reciprocated, rearing and knocking Cloud backward. Undeterred, the brassy colt bit at

the yearling's mane, and the two nipped at each other's legs and spun in a circle. When play got rougher, the palomino moved in, laying her ears back. The yearling understood the subtle reprimand immediately and trotted away. Cloud stood and watched him go, and then he walked over and began nursing his mother as if nothing had happened.

In the dying light, mule deer emerged from the trees, grazing at the edges of the meadows near Cloud's family. As a full moon edged over the Bighorn Mountains, a chorus of coyote voices echoed across the mountaintop. How many were there? One or two can sound like a dozen. Their excited, high-pitched yips came from the direction of the teacup bowl. I glanced over at Cloud to see if he was listening. Together we turned in the direction of the calls.

Raven whinnied his most ear-piercing call and charged after his band, every muscle in his body rippling.

FOUR

The Theft

The flowers were profuse in Cloud's first summer. The purple lupine had spread across the meadows on top of the mountain. Scattered among them were magenta shooting stars, white fuzzy bistort, and flax. Yellow stonecrop and bright blue forget-me-nots grew along the rocky cliff edges. Mountain bluebirds hovered in the stiff breezes and then swooped low and landed to pick up insects. Marmots groomed themselves on the sunny limestone outcrops, and a golden eagle soared high, taking note of the marmots below.

As the days grew hotter, the water hole below the shrinking snowfield became a magnet for the bands. Some of the bands trailed in across the snowfield with the foals slipping and sliding to the bottom like beginner skiers on a bunny slope. Smaller groups came and drank and left while Raven's dominant band took its time. On the longest day of the year, I watched Cloud and his sisters race to the water, followed by the mares and then by Diamond. But Raven wandered off to flex his muscles with a group of bachelors. Some of the band stallions loved to cavort with the young males, playing like colts.

While Raven's mares drank, a blood-bay stallion named King trotted over the hill and stopped to look at the leaderless band. King was a former band stallion who had lost his mares to another stallion, and he was not in a good mood. He had buddied up with a three-year-old grulla bachelor. In tandem, they moved toward Raven's mares. I looked around for Raven, but he and the bachelors had disappeared into a small canyon below the water hole. Diamond was grazing near the pond while Smokey and Mahogany waded in the shallows. Cloud was busy investigating bees in a bed of lupines. That's when the stallions rushed in.

King and the grulla charged the group, their heads laid low with ears flattened. Smokey's mother, Grumpy, signaled the group, swiveling in place and striking out at the bay with a hind foot. The claybank kicked out as she ran away from the big grulla

A bee does its work in a bed of lupines—an activity that Cloud finds worthy of investigation.

stallion. The foals ran alongside their mothers, knowing instinctively this was the safest place to be. The palomino broke out of the pack. With Cloud hugging her side, she dashed up the hill to evade the stallions. But the bay snaked her back.

Much as they tried to fend off the stallions, the three mares were no match for two adult males. The stallion got the band all going together in the right direction, which was away from Raven. I looked downhill, expecting to see the black stallion coming, but he was nowhere to be seen. When I looked back at the fleeing band, I saw King lash out at the grulla bachelor with his teeth bared. The grulla immediately retreated, leaving King with the entire band.

That's when mild-mannered Diamond did the unexpected, what I'm sure his father would have done if he hadn't been off playing with the bachelors. He ran in front of King to head him off, turned his rear end to the stallion, and kicked with all his might. He nearly threw himself off his feet when his hooves connected with nothing but air. Regaining his balance, he wheeled around to face King. The bay, who was twice Diamond's size, didn't miss a beat. He ran at the little yearling, driving him backward out of his way. Diamond staggered and King raced at the heels of the band. But Diamond caught up with him again, cutting him off and momentarily slowing him down.

Raven scans the landscape,
looking for any dangers that
may threaten him or his band.

Marmots groomed themselves on the sunny limestone outcrops, and a golden eagle soared high, taking note of the marmots below.

Then I saw Raven rushing back to the water hole. He looked back and forth nervously, prancing and tossing his head. He glanced up just in time to see his family disappearing over the hill. Raven whinnied his most ear-piercing call and charged after them, every muscle in his body rippling. Faster and faster he galloped to the top of the hill. He whinnied again and ran out of sight. The next sounds were the earsplitting battle cries of stallions. Raven had caught up to the bay and was fighting for his family.

In what seemed like less than a minute, I saw Cloud, Smokey, Mahogany, and Diamond running full speed up a distant slope. They were working hard to keep up with their mothers. Then I saw Raven in the rear, driving them all away. The black stallion had reclaimed his family faster than they had been stolen. His band stopped running and glanced back toward the water hole. King trotted back to the water's edge and took a long drink. Whether the older stallion felt the sting of defeat, I'll never know. It didn't keep him from continuing to try to find a mare. By summer's end he would succeed—but not at Raven's expense.

*Fog can swallow up the landscape
in a matter of minutes, dropping
temperatures twenty or thirty degrees.*

FIVE

Lost in
the Fog

In late summer, the grass turned yellowish brown. Most of the horses had traveled several miles to the west to higher meadows where more snow had fallen over the winter and the drifts had lingered longer. Out here, the grass was still green, especially on the edges of the forest clearings.

The snow-fed water hole was a drying mud hole now, so the watering place of choice was a small, spring-fed lake near these high meadows. It was surrounded on three sides by Douglas firs. The clear little lake was a great place to find traces of just about every animal on the Arrowheads heavy enough to make tracks along the muddy bank. Coyote and deer tracks were common; even an occasional bear track could be found. Ravens, nutcrackers, and tiny birds such as mountain chickadees and chipping sparrows left their delicate footprints.

As I walked around the perimeter, the track that caught my eye this day in late summer was a big one, bigger than any coyote's. I bent down and placed my hand in the print. The paw was wider than my hand and, even in the soft mud, the indentations made by the claws were subtle. "Mountain lion," I whispered and looked over my shoulder into the dark forest. A large cat could creep out of the dense trees and deadfall for a drink and then melt back into the cover without being detected. Was he still there, his golden eyes peering out at me from behind a log? I stood up. Crouched over, I might have looked like a perfect four-legged meal.

From the pond, I walked far out on what are called *islands*—meadows and forest isolated on three sides by steep canyon walls. The walls are pockmarked with caves, which make perfect places for mountain lions to den. Combined with a big mule deer population, this was ideal cougar country. The wind picked up and low clouds began rolling through the trees into the open meadows. Fog can swallow up the landscape in a matter of minutes, dropping temperatures twenty or thirty degrees. I pulled the collar up on my jacket and slipped on my gloves and hat.

In the distance, I could make out Raven's band grazing in a little valley that was peppered with tight circles of fir trees. I didn't see the foals right away, which always gave me a start. Hopefully, Cloud was less vulnerable to a cat attack now than when he had been a frail newborn. Through the grove of trees, I spotted a flash of

Canyon walls pockmarked with caves combine with a big mule deer population to make this ideal cougar country.

white and knew Cloud was safe. As I rounded the trees, I saw that all three foals had imprudently wandered quite close to a red roan stallion and his mares.

The roan walked toward them with his neck arched, lifting each front leg exaggeratedly high like a fancy dressage horse. To diffuse his aggression, Cloud and his sisters lowered their heads and began to open and close their mouths rapidly, a submissive gesture called *teeth clacking. I'm sorry, forgive me*, the three seemed to mouth in unison. The stallion laid back his ears and drove them off a few steps. The three continued opening and closing their mouths. Before the roan could make another run at the foals, Raven rushed in and gave him a threatening look, freezing the roan in his tracks. Then Raven laid his ears back, lowered his head, and snaked his wandering foals back home.

Cloud raced in front, not one bit repentant. Instead, he used the opportunity for a good sprint. His mother nickered softly to him, and he trotted over to nurse. I imagined it was not the first time that Raven had retrieved his adventuresome trio. No sooner were the foals safely back than the fog rolled in thick and gray. It was so dense that I lost sight of the band. I began to make my way back to the road.

Long ago I learned to pay attention not only to where I was going but also to where I'd been. I learned to look over my shoulder every so often so I could backtrack and not get lost on the way home. Even so, everything looked so different in the fog. Distant landmarks were invisible, so I relied on familiar stands of trees, a pile of rocks, a deep gully, horse trails, and even stud piles for navigational markers.

Wild horse stallions defecate on each other's droppings. Over time, accumulated droppings can make a conspicuous, cone-shaped mound several feet tall. Nearly every stallion passing by will add to the pile, leaving a sort of personalized calling card. The next stallion will know who is in the area and can even assess the health of the depositor. While stud piles mean little to me in an olfactory sense, this time they helped me find my way out to the road safely.

It would be nearly two years before I would walk those wilderness trails again in the hopes of finding Cloud.

*Raven's band and other family
groups gather at a spring-fed
water hole late in the summer.*

SIX

The Bears

My work took me around the world, filming animals in exotic places in Asia and Africa. No matter where I traveled, though, I never forgot Cloud. I wondered if he was alive and well. In every season I tried to imagine where he was and what he might be doing. Was the snow deep? Did he have enough to eat? Did he have new brothers or sisters? These were all questions I hoped to answer when I returned.

In late May, around the time of Cloud's second birthday, I traveled back to the Arrowheads, hoping to find Cloud and Raven, the palomino and Diamond. My four-wheeler lurched up the old rocky road. I stopped, reached for my binoculars, and began to glass the windswept ridges. I could make out a few horses in the distance, but none were Raven's band or Cloud. I drove on. At the teacup-shaped bowl, I stopped and looked east toward the Bighorns and saw light-colored horses a mile or two away. Was one of them Cloud? I grabbed my binoculars. It was Raven's band, but Cloud wasn't with them; neither were Smokey or Mahogany. It was the palomino mother who flashed in the sun. I could make out three foals and several yearlings.

Again, I slid on the greasy road to get closer, stopping on my way to unpack some of my gear at a little old cabin that became as familiar to me as an old friend. When Cloud was a baby, I had camped here often. I ducked down to avoid hitting my head on the top of the low doorframe as I carried my equipment in and set it down. The sign above the door read *Penn's Cabin*, for the young cowboy, Perrin Cummings, who had built it back in the 1920s. Perrin went by the nickname Penn, which was appropriate because he was an accomplished writer of prose and poetry.

I propped open the wooden shutters, and light streamed in the south-facing windows. A whinny and the sound of pounding hooves pulled me out of the cabin and into the bright light of a spring day.

Several bands were drinking and rolling in a muddy red water hole not one hundred yards from the cabin. I walked out and watched the dun stallion, Shaman, and his band.

> *Several bands were drinking and rolling in a muddy red water hole not one hundred yards from the cabin. I walked out and watched the dun stallion, Shaman, and his band.*

The experienced stallion had done well for himself since the roundup of 1994 when he and his big band were captured. While Shaman was held in the corrals at the base of the mountain, some of his mares were released back to the wild. Weeks later, Shaman was released. By that time, his mares had been picked up by other stallions, so Shaman had to start over again and rebuild his band from scratch.

Now he had five mares, including a brown roan filly who looked to be a two-year-old. When she turned my way, I recognized the shape of the star on her head. *Mahogany.* I smiled. Cloud's sturdy sister had chosen one of my favorite stallions. Shaman was a nurturing male who showed great affection for his family. It was common to see him and his mares and yearlings huddled together in a tight little pack, switching pesky flies off each other while the foals lay stretched at their feet, soaking up the summer sun.

Suddenly, Shaman blew air out of his nose with a loud, explosive blast that startled me. He whirled and blew again. I stooped down with my binoculars in hand. Shaman had snorted at me once like this when he didn't know who I was. But I wasn't the object of his agitation this time. I looked at the grove of firs that held Shaman's attention. At first, it looked like just a bunch of trees. Then I saw movement. A black bear was standing on his hind legs right in front of the dark trunks. He was stretched up on his tiptoes, trying to see over the little rise that separated him from Shaman. The bear, who looked to be about two years old, had no doubt been on his way to the little water hole when Shaman snorted. The young bear sniffed the air and dropped on all fours. Turning in my direction, he put his nose in the air and sniffed again. He pivoted his compact body and disappeared into the trees. He'd caught my scent.

I waited a few seconds before following the bear. I skirted the trees and walked along the edge of a steep cliff, hoping to catch another glimpse of him. The narrow valley beneath the steep drop-off formed the headwaters of Layout Creek, a little trickle that eventually emptied into the Bighorn River thousands of feet below. The bear must have navigated the steep slope into the valley, for he was nowhere to be seen.

Scanning the distant upper reaches of the valley, I was surprised to see another bear about a mile away, a beautiful cinnamon one, perhaps the young bear's mother, for she

Suddenly, Shaman blew air out of his nose with a loud, explosive blast. He whirled and blew again. A black bear was the object of his agitation.

looked larger. Her head was buried in the grass, and I imagined she was digging for roots. Shaman snorted again, and I jerked around to see him tearing off with Mahogany and the band. No one could snort quite as explosively as Shaman could. When I turned back, the cinnamon bear had disappeared. That was my first encounter with bears on the Arrowheads, but it would not be my last—not by a long shot.

I walked to the muddy red water hole, where I could get a good view of the broad meadows atop the mountain. About a quarter of a mile away, I saw Raven and the mares. As I walked closer, I could see that the black stallion looked wonderful, just as magnificent as the last time I had seen him. And the three mares looked sleek and healthy. Each had a foal. The little claybank buckskin mare had a red roan filly with a lightning-bolt mark on her face. Grumpy had a burly grulla colt who looked a lot like her. And the palomino had a little buckskin filly, Cloud's sister. The two yearlings in the band were both males, a red roan with a broken blaze, and a yellow buckskin who had to be Cloud's brother. I named the beautiful buckskin Yellow Fox.

Much as I enjoyed watching the yearlings groom and spar with each other while the foals played, I missed seeing Cloud and Diamond and his sisters all together. Mahogany was with Shaman. But where were the others? Where were Smokey and Diamond? And where was Cloud?

I scoured the open meadows but didn't see him. Raven no doubt had kicked Diamond and Cloud out of the band when the mares came in heat. If my hunch was right, Diamond had been a bachelor for a full year now while Cloud had been on his own just for the last few months. He would have found companionship with other bachelors. Young males form rowdy gangs of troublemakers, rebellious teenagers with no responsibilities who can and do go wherever they want. That's what makes them so hard to find.

Young males form rowdy gangs of troublemakers, rebellious teenagers with no responsibilities who can and do go wherever they want.

Mutual grooming is reserved for friends such as these two bachelor stallions.

SEVEN

The Bachelors

I decided to drive down from the mountaintop to an open spot below the deep forest. I drove into the meadows on Tillet Ridge, where Cloud had been born. On a high vantage point, I set up my spotting scope on a tripod and began the tedious job of looking for Cloud, scanning each ridge and valley one small piece at a time.

When I didn't see any horses on Tillet, I trained my scope across the deep, impassable canyon called Big Coulee. I began to look across the canyon to an even bigger ridge called Sykes. Both Tillet and Sykes Ridges eventually join like craggy fingers atop the mountain. Sykes is immense. It took me a long time to pan across its many canyons and meadows. Toward the top of Sykes, just below the line of densest trees, I saw a group of horses, including a light-colored one. When the sun broke from under the cloud cover, the horse shone white in the brilliant light. It was Cloud. It had to be. He was alive!

Excitedly, I tried to work out how to get closer. There was too much snow in the trees on upper Sykes to drive over the top and then down. The only alternative I had was to drive down one ridge and up the other. It would take hours with no guarantee that Cloud would be anywhere near there when I arrived. I tried to memorize the landscape where the bachelors were grazing. I wanted to be sure I could find the exact finger of land and distinguish it from the dozens of look-alikes.

Five hours and twenty incredibly tough miles later, I stopped where I could look out onto the ridge that I thought was the one. As luck would have it, I had found the right one. Luckier still, the bachelors hadn't moved off of it. When I couldn't see Cloud in the group, I

I watched the bachelors for hours as they ran and kicked up their heels and then stopped to graze and take short naps while standing.

walked out on the long finger, hoping a different angle would yield a glimpse of him. In the distance, he stepped from behind a grove of trees with twisted trunks. The closer I got, the better he looked, with his coat shining in the sun. Nearly two years ago to the day, I had watched Cloud totter from the trees as a newborn foal.

When he looked up and saw me, I stopped and waved. Would he remember the two-legged who meant no harm and always announced her presence by flailing her arm in the air? He stood still and watched, and so did I. Then he went back to grazing. I moved closer and sat down quietly on a log. Through my binoculars, I could appreciate what a beauty he was. His mane and tail were white, and his body was nearly so—more a very light cream color. The hair on his back legs had grown just a little darker, more the palomino color of his mother. He was taller and sturdier looking than the two-year-old dun stallion at his side.

The older stallions in the group of six started to play, biting on one another's necks and legs. That was the only encouragement Cloud needed to initiate a play bout with his dun companion. Around and around they spun, gently biting on each other's manes

The older stallions in the group of six started to play, biting on one another's necks and legs.

and tails, then rearing up only to drop down onto their knees. Each bit at the other's pasterns. The play of Cloud and the two-year-old underscored the importance of friends and family to wild horses. In this, wild horses and humans are not so different. I watched the bachelors for hours as they ran and kicked up their heels, then stopped to graze and take short naps while standing. Horses can lock their joints and sleep standing up so they are ready to run if danger presents itself.

Within several days, Cloud and his bachelor buddies from Sykes Ridge had climbed through the forest to the top of the mountain. From Penn's cabin I saw them coming, so I hiked to get a better view. The young stallions marched next to one another. As they crossed a meadow sprinkled with family bands, they dropped into single file. Stallion fathers moved out of their bands to warn the bachelors, striking defiant poses that meant *keep your distance if you know what's good for you.* The bachelors obliged, walking to the far side of the big meadow and then out of sight.

I followed as best I could. The top of Arrowhead Mountain is flat in places but broken by shallow canyons and undulating hills. Horses on the move, even at a walk, can far outdistance a human at a walk, especially on uneven ground. The bachelors crisscrossed a high plain, then dropped down into the forest on a narrow trail, emerging onto the side of another treeless slope. In the distance, I saw a group of horses above them. They were watching the bachelors. When I trained my binoculars on the group, I could see Diamond on the hilltop, his mane blowing in the stiff breeze.

I wondered why Cloud had chosen to go over to Sykes, far from his birthplace and his bachelor brother. Perhaps when Raven expelled him from the family they had been in the desert lowlands, where there is a mixing of horses from both ridges. Maybe the nearest bachelor Cloud found had grown up on Sykes Ridge. So when the weather warmed up and the snow melted, he followed that bachelor up the ridge. In any case, the bachelors were all getting back together, and sparks began to fly.

The greeting of stallions is ritualized and thrilling to watch. One by one, the young males touched noses and jerked their heads back with piercing screams. Then they whirled around, and one defecated, followed by the other. Each then smelled the droppings of the other and spun around and kicked and screamed again. Cloud tried to

match the skills of the older stallions but seemed unable to defecate on the droppings of another. I had to laugh as he missed the target by a foot or more. Diamond, on the other hand, was more practiced and a dead shot.

Once all these formalities were taken care of, the whole group grazed together like the best of friends. I watched Cloud interact with Diamond, scratching Diamond's neck and back with his teeth. And Diamond did the same to Cloud. Mutual grooming is reserved for good friends and, in this case, for half brothers too.

By midsummer, I noticed that Cloud was starting to assert himself more, to play more of a leadership role in the bachelor band. Yet this seemed unlikely for a two-year-old. Late in the day, I sat above the spring-fed water hole and watched the bands coming to water. Cloud and a group of ten bachelors barreled down the hillside, kicking up their heels as they skidded to a stop on the shore. They drank, pawed, and played in the water, and then they rolled in the dirt. All except Cloud, that is. I hardly ever saw him dirty. Was he proud of his pristine light coat?

As the young males left the lake, Shaman and Mahogany and the band trailed in through the forest. Instead of respectfully backing off, Cloud boldly trotted up to the big stallion and kicked out at his head. I gasped, fearing Cloud was in for it. But before the startled stallion could react, Cloud dashed off up the hill and started to graze nonchalantly. Surprisingly, Shaman let him go. Cloud's brashness was consistent with his behavior as a foal; the bold foal had grown into a reckless adolescent.

The bachelor band moved far out into forest meadows, leaving Cloud behind. He may not have noticed that they had left because he was nibbling intently on some short shoots of grass. When he looked up and saw he was the only bachelor around, he didn't run after his friends as I'd seen others do. Instead, he stood on the hilltop and whinnied. I could hear the distant replies of the bachelors. Cloud whinnied again, and

The greeting of stallions is ritualized and thrilling to watch. One by one, the young males touched noses and jerked their heads back with piercing screams.

Late in the day, I sat above the spring-fed water hole and watched as Cloud barreled down the hillside.

the replies grew closer. In a few minutes, the whole group of bachelors had come back to get him, and off they trotted in the opposite direction. How did he get them to do that? Did Cloud hold some special power over his friends? Do some animals have a special magnetism that commands respect? I wondered.

In August, I sat on a rock bleached white as bone and watched the bands move out to the higher meadows. The horses seemed such wonderful reminders of a time when extravagant herds of bison, mammoths, giant sloths, and wild horses once roamed the land. Did the first humans to come here sit on this same rock? Did they see the rolling hills of what is now the Crow Indian Reservation to the north? Did they see the tops of the Bighorn Mountains to the east?

I was roused out of my daydream by a sharp scream, and then another. Before I saw them, I knew who was coming. A dozen bachelors raced into view across meadows ablaze with late summer stands of death camas and bistort. The young stallions only added to the color of the summer day. They were jet black, seal brown, golden dun, and steely grulla. They were blue roans, one red, and, of course, one white horse.

As they played, I noticed Diamond and the five-year-old sorrel bachelor sparring, their play escalating into a full-fledged contest of strength. They slammed their butts into each other and started pushing like well-matched wrestlers. Then they started kicking with their back legs. I winced at the thud of hooves hitting flesh. Dust flew as they kicked and screamed. As a three-year-old, Diamond was showing the spunk that might one day make him a powerful band stallion like his father. Not all bachelors have what it takes to win and hold mares. Some barely make the effort, while others nearly die trying. I was convinced Diamond would succeed in starting his own family.

When Cloud came over to join the fight, Diamond turned on him and snaked him up the hill as though he were a mare. Sometimes older stallions will pick a young bachelor and practice their herding techniques as if he were a she. Cloud didn't seem to mind, keeping his cool and wandering off to graze with his dun companion.

Cloud looked up when a coyote sprinted through the meadow behind him. The grayish-red coyote stopped and looked back over her shoulder toward me. Maybe she saw me sitting on the hill because she started running, carrying one leg in the air. Had she been shot or caught in a trap? Thousands of coyotes were unfairly targeted every year. Even here, where they so perfectly fit into the wilderness environment, they could be shot. The crippled coyote disappeared into dense Douglas firs.

Cloud went back to grazing, taking no notice of the mule deer moving from the forest. Big bucks with their huge velvety racks wandered cautiously from cover to graze the forest edges. A marmot called from a nearby outcrop. Water pipits chirped and hopped from rock to rock as kestrels hovered and dove, landing to pluck grasshoppers from among the camas. How I loved this place and the wild creatures who lived here. It seemed so perfect and peaceful. Soon, so much would change.

EIGHT

The Roundup

A golden eagle launched itself off a high cliff and flew north, away from the Arrowheads. Another "big bird" was moving in, a helicopter that struck fear in the hearts of the horses. The Bureau of Land Management (BLM) was beginning its roundup.

The bands began to run as the helicopter swept low over their heads, driving them from the mountaintop, through the forest, over the windswept meadows, down through the canyons, and out onto the red desert flats.

I hid behind a fence constructed atop a mesa about half a mile from the wings of a trap. Wide at the mouth, the trap gradually narrowed like a funnel, emptying into metal corrals at the base of the mountain. Band after band rushed through the red desert with the helicopter nipping at their heels. When they were within the wings of the trap, a wrangler released a tall bay horse who was trained to run for the corrals. A horse used for this purpose is aptly named a Judas horse because he betrays his own species. The wild horses see one of their own and follow him, not to safety, but to confinement.

I dreaded this day and prayed that Cloud could evade capture. I watched as Plenty Coups and his band scrambled up a sandy arroyo but were cut off and redirected by the savvy chopper pilot. Jim Hicks had piloted helicopters in Vietnam and was used to dangerous missions. He had rounded up thousands of wild horses all over the West, and there was none better. As Plenty Coups approached the wings, I saw that Smokey was in his band. Cloud's lovely black-brown sister was leading the way. Little did she know where her path would end. Once Plenty Coups's band was captured, the helicopter wheeled around and went looking for more horses. Shaman was captured and Mahogany with him.

The old sorrel stallion, Flash, came running in along with his bay lieutenant stallion, a chestnut roan mare, and her yearling blue roan son. Flash and the bay had formed an unlikely team when they stole the mare and her son from another band stallion. From then on, the bay was in charge of fighting off any challengers, while Flash spent time with the mare and yearling.

I enjoyed watching them come to the water hole. Flash and the yearling clearly loved the water. They would lie down side by side and roll and roll in the shallow muddy water. The yearling was one of the only horses I had ever seen lie in water and totally immerse his head.

In my mind, he was the most beautiful of the yearlings on the Arrowheads, a lovely blue-gray color with a jet-black head and legs and one tiny white coronet band just above his back hoof. He had a strong head with soft, wide-set eyes.

The four horses had slowed a bit. I think Flash sensed the danger ahead, for the old stallion had been captured many times over the years, but never before by a helicopter. Just then, the wrangler released the Judas horse and he raced away, flying by Flash's band. Glancing over, the bay lieutenant stallion saw the Judas horse pass and picked up the pace, attempting to catch up. Flash and his little band galloped headlong through the gate. Men hiding behind the fencing rushed out, waving plastic bags on the ends of whips, and closed the big gate behind them.

Again the helicopter turned and flew low over the pale orange hills and deep red buttes, and then it disappeared. I could hear the clatter of the propeller grow fainter. Then, ever so slowly, the sound grew louder. More horses must have been found not too far out among the deep arroyos and scant junipers. In time, I could see the chopper was driving in a group that had no foals or yearlings. They were bachelors. And not just any bachelors, but the Sykes Ridge band, the duns and grullas, the little black, and Cloud. I could barely watch as they entered the wings of the trap and frantically ran toward the corrals. When the gate closed behind them, their freedom was swept away.

In the afternoon, the BLM crew let us visit the pens that housed the horses. With tears in my eyes, I looked in to see Smokey and Mahogany walking aimlessly about in a daze. Wild horses look pathetic in captivity. I'm convinced they are in a state of depression. They have lost what they value most, their freedom and their family. I walked to the corral where Cloud and his friends were confined. Cloud turned to stare at me. "There's nothing I can do, boy," I whispered. I realized that these young stallions would never again run across flower-strewn meadows in a mad and carefree dash to the water hole. They would never again explore the wild meadows and forested canyons that were their home. And they would never have the chance to win a mare or father their own wild horse babies. I was unbelievably sad and could only turn away.

Late in the day, Cloud was isolated in his own corral. He whinnied for his friends, who answered. He paced and called and paced. But they would never be reunited.

I realized that these young stallions would never again run free with the wildlife, such as these bighorn sheep, and explore the wild meadows and forested canyons that were their home.

Of the bachelors captured, only Cloud was singled out for release. As a two-year-old, Cloud was a prime candidate for sale, but his unusual coat color bought him a ticket to freedom. I believe the BLM hoped that if he became a band stallion, he might pass on his beautiful light coat color to his foals.

Band stallions and their lead mares and some of the other reproducing mares and their foals were also scheduled for release. But young animals, over the age of one and under the age of five, are more likely to be purchased by the public. Most of these youngsters were not released back to the wild.

The BLM workers ran Cloud through a shoot, pulling hair samples for later DNA testing. They then painted a blue line down his back so the helicopter pilot could tell he was not to be recaptured.

The next day, the BLM allowed some of us to hide behind the fence near the corrals as they opened the gate. Flash tore out of the gate, followed by his mare, and then a stocky bay stallion named Mateo with his mare. Finally, hesitantly, Cloud came out. The two-year-old didn't belong in the company of band stallions with mares, and he knew it. Mateo lagged back, laying his ears back as he ran at Cloud, who dodged out of the way. Cloud dropped back, following at an acceptable distance until they cleared the wings of the trap and disappeared into the desert.

Cloud's bachelor friends were prepared for sale along with his sisters, Smokey and Mahogany, and Flash's blue roan yearling. They were freeze-branded with a number on their necks—unique symbols that allowed for their identification. On a cold and gloomy fall day, they were auctioned off.

Most buyers came from nearby ranches. They might gentle their wild horses for riding. Some were bought for breeding. Others would be kept for one year, until the buyer received legal ownership from the government. Then the horses could be sold. Sadly, some horses are purchased by killer buyers who haul them to slaughterhouses. Horsemeat is highly desirable in some European countries as well as in Japan, and there is money to be made in trafficking horses.

While most of the wild horse buyers came from the local area, one came from Colorado. I became a wild horse owner. If the blue roan yearling couldn't go free, I would try to give him the next best thing: a home on my little ranch in the Sangre de Cristo Mountains of southern Colorado. Smokey and Mahogany were bought by local people but later went to live with my best friend and her son on a beautiful ranch in Florida.

I named my yearling Absarokee Trace—Absarokee for the proud Crow Indians who once claimed all the Arrowheads as their sacred land. The white man named the tall, handsome native people Crows, though they called themselves the Absarokee, meaning Children of the Big Beaked-Bird. The bird was either a crow or, more likely, a raven. I shortened the colt's name to Trace.

Trace has many meanings that seemed appropriate for this likely descendent of Indian horses. A trace can be a path or trail, such as the Natchez Trace, or it can mean the sign of evidence of something in the past. He will always hold a special place in my heart, and I am proud to say he is mine. But another part of me will always wish he had been allowed to live free on the Arrowheads. With his confident, commanding personality, I believe Trace would have become a band stallion.

I began the process of gentling Trace, slowly and with patience. Wild and distrustful at first, he came to understand that I was not to be feared. He also learned that he couldn't intimidate me as he had the wild yearlings that were held with him when they were captured. Trace kept them away from the hay bunk simply by laying his ears back and glaring at them.

In time, we developed a great friendship. I made him a promise. "Someday," I said, "we'll go home to the Arrowheads, you and I. Just for a visit. Would you like that, big guy?" I rubbed his face at the little place just below his eyes that he liked. His lids closed halfway, and I thought I heard him sigh.

*Wild and distrustful at first, Trace came
to understand that I was not to be feared.
In time, we developed a great friendship.*

NINE

The Search

Fall had been kind to the horses in Raven's band. They were never rounded up. I found them at the snow-fed water hole atop the mountain, now a muddy puddle in a sea of brown grass. Other horses who were not sold or who had evaded capture reclaimed the golden meadows for the last peaceful weeks of autumn.

Raven's three foals cantered into the limber pines to rub on downed logs and low-hanging branches. Clark's nutcrackers flew in and out of the trees above the foals. The noisy gray-and-white birds were busy gathering their supply of nuts from the limber pines. Gullets bulging, they flew off to cache the nuts in small cracks in the cliffs. This reliable winter food supply allows the nutcrackers to nest early, when the forests and meadows are still in the grip of winter.

I caught a glimpse of a pair of coyotes running playfully through the pines. They were running in the direction of the teacup bowl. Effortlessly, they jumped over logs at the edge of the trees and broke into the clear, crisscrossing through the sage on the open hillside. Ravens cawed and circled, landing in small flocks. They plucked grasshoppers from the brittle grass and then waddled on. And from high in the deep blue fall sky, a golden eagle surveyed it all, made a lazy turn, and flew away.

I found Diamond and his bachelor band in a forest opening halfway up Tillet Ridge. They were playing in a dusting of early snow that had fallen the night before. I believe that Diamond and his group had been far out in the western meadows and canyons during the roundup. They were outside the designated borders of the horse range, where they were safe from the helicopter. Whether luck or instinct had saved Diamond from the fate of the other bachelors, I'll never know.

And what of Cloud? He seemed to have vanished from the Arrowheads. I searched everywhere I had ever seen him. I walked back into Big Coulee, the canyon that separates Sykes from Tillet Ridge. I stared up at walls that gradually rise hundreds of feet high and have fir trees clinging precariously on their sides. The farther back I walked, the narrower the canyon became. It became so narrow that I could stretch my arms to the sides and touch both walls at once. Here I found the tracks of a lone horse, but I couldn't tell Cloud's hoofprints from any of the others.

I went back to the top of the mountain and found mountain lion tracks in the mud depression that was once the snow-fed water hole. An eerie silence wrapped around me. Winter was coming, and I feared Cloud was alone for the first time in his life.

There was more snow than normal that winter. It covered the Arrowheads from top to bottom and made looking for horses tough. I drove up on Tillet Ridge as far as I could go and found a black stallion named Boomer and his little band. I walked uphill but ran into deep drifts. The absence of tracks convinced me that there were no horses higher up.

In the upper desert area, a band of horses with ice hanging from their manes and tails were pawing at the sandy cliff sides. They were enlarging tiny depressions, turning them into minicaves. They reached their noses into the holes and licked the loosened dirt. Particularly mares crave the minerals in these yellow rocks.

At the very bottom of the horse range, Raven and his band were eking out a living on the scant vegetation they dug from beneath a half a foot of snow. Even at lower elevations, the temperature dipped well below zero, yet the band seemed to be holding its own on a combination of weeds and determination. More so than domestic cattle and sheep, horses are able to maintain themselves on a poor-quality diet that is high in fiber.

Over the next few months, I started to hunt for Cloud in areas where I'd never seen him. With binoculars, I carefully scanned the rugged cliffs and exposed ridges of the remote Lost Water Canyon area to the west of the horse range. Two bands were rumored to live up in this snowy citadel all year round, but I saw no clue of Cloud or any other wild horses. I looked in the area of the Bighorn Canyon and found bighorn sheep digging through the snow for tufts of grass and nibbling on the berries and leaves of juniper bushes. A herd of mule deer ran to higher slopes when they saw me coming. I found a few lean horses who live here all the time, but no Cloud. Sunrises came late and sunsets came early, making for frustratingly short, unsuccessful days of searching.

In early May, the high country was still locked in snow and inaccessible, so I hiked the desert again and made a horrible discovery. Lying next to a barbed wire fence, I found the body of Cloud's buckskin brother, the yearling I had named Yellow Fox. Though he was badly decomposed, I recognized his beautiful buckskin coat with

the black mane and tail. Yellow Fox had been a new, inexperienced bachelor, not yet two years old. He was no doubt looking for other bachelors to join up with. In his haste, he appeared to have run right into the fence. I bent down and looked at the ground where he had pawed a trench in his struggle to free himself from the wire. I touched the black hair entangled in its barbs. I knew the death of this lovely Raven son had been a long and excruciating one, and so pointless. There was no need for interior fences on the range, not since cattle had been outlawed from here in the 1970s, yet the BLM had never removed them. If I possessed the power and authority to tear them down, that is exactly what I would have done. I prayed that Cloud had not suffered a similar fate.

By late May, I feared the worst. I imagined Cloud had been stolen by horse thieves or killed by a mountain lion. Maybe he had slipped off an icy cliff and died. Around the time of his birthday, I was able to drive up Tillet Ridge to the top of the mountain. As in years past, the family bands were following the greening of the grass and the melting of the snow. I watched Plenty Coups run down to drink at the snow-fed water hole. Even though Smokey had been taken from him, the beautiful blue roan stallion still had a band of nine, including a new foal. King ran down the hill with his grulla mare and yearling, followed by Shaman and his band. The horses were in high spirits on this cool day. Even the adults ran and bucked like foals.

Lying next to a barbed wire fence, I found the badly decomposed body of Cloud's buckskin brother, who I had named Yellow Fox.

Farther away, a big group of horses broke over the hill. In the middle of a band of bachelors was Cloud! He stood out like a bright light in a sea of dark horses. He was alive, safe, and running to the water hole! What a sight for sore eyes—Cloud! Diamond was there, too, and Cloud's half brother, the red roan colt I had named Red Raven. There must have been a dozen of them, kicking up their heels, jumping rocks, and dodging holes—new bachelors combined with those, like Diamond, who had evaded the helicopter. Cloud was one of the first horses into the water, followed by a dozen others. I was overjoyed to see him but sad, too. How Yellow Fox would have loved to share the joy of the moment with these young stallions!

The big stallion Two Boots came to the water while his family waited on the hill. He went to Diamond first, nudging him out of the way. Then he picked on Cloud, who walked uphill a ways, but the big stallion pursued him, biting on his neck. That's when Cloud came to life. He reared up a bit as he squealed and pushed on the bigger horse. The black pushed back, but Cloud had the higher ground and shoved the stallion down the dusty hill. Then Cloud calmly walked a few steps away. This was the first time I'd seen Cloud in a direct confrontation with a mature stallion, and he was impressive. Here was another Raven son who showed real band stallion potential.

I moved in closer and sat down among the shooting stars, low-growing flax, and greening grass. Cloud would never know what a relief it was for me to see him. I studied the muscles rippling under his white coat. He had the same soft eyes and beautiful head with a little pink cross on his nose. He might have the powerful personality of his father, but he looked so like his mother. His coat had a few nicks; otherwise, he was perfection.

As the first day of summer approached, Cloud and the other young stallions grew more and more restless. It was near the end of the foaling season, and most mares were coming into heat. Band stallions were on high alert, guarding their mares from potential thieves. For the most part, the bachelors didn't push these mature stallions. Instead, they watched for an opportunity to abduct an unguarded mare or young filly who had left her band. Open warfare with a bigger, stronger stallion could end in a serious injury or even, in rare instances, death.

TEN

Electra

About a quarter of a mile east of the snow-fed waterhole, Raven's band was grazing peacefully when I noticed one of his fillies wander away from her buckskin mother and the rest of the band. Of all the young females on the mountain, this filly, who I named Electra, was clearly the flashiest. Her red roan body and orange mane and tail were set off by an amazing lightning-bolt zigzag pattern on her face. A small, feminine head fit perfectly on her delicate but sturdy frame. Her yearling brother Gray Bear watched his beautiful sister move away. Where did she think she was going?

Electra carried her orange tail slightly elevated, and I spotted a little discharge underneath it. The filly was in heat, probably for the first time. She walked slowly in the direction of the bay stallion King, who had stolen Raven's band three years before. This seemed odd. Most fillies venture outside the protective confines of their family band when they are two or even three years old, but not as yearlings—at least, not in my experience. Yet she was clearly soliciting King's attention. Bachelor stallions, including Cloud, stood rapt on the hill.

King lifted his head and nickered softly to Electra. Walking up to her, he touched her nose then sniffed her ears and her sides. Calmly and gently, he mounted the filly. *This isn't a good thing*, I thought. If her brazen behavior produced a foal in a year's time, the foal would likcly die; plus, the energy needed to carry a pregnancy through winter might forever stunt Electra's growth. Like her older brothers Diamond and Cloud, Electra's boldness seemed typical of Raven's offspring. Was this precociousness inherited or learned? It was probably a combination of both. I hoped it wouldn't jeopardize Electra's life.

Gray Bear whinnied to his sister and then took a chance and came to join her and King. He clacked his teeth the entire time, hoping to diffuse any anger from the older stallion. It seemed to work. King touched noses with Gray Bear and then allowed him and Electra to walk back toward their family. By the time they were halfway back, Raven had noticed the two were gone and was already on his way to collect them. But as soon as Electra returned, she wandered off again.

By the time Gray Bear and Electra
were halfway back, Raven had
noticed the two were gone and was
already on his way to collect them.

*Cloud and the bachelors stood rapt
on the hill, watching Electra solicit the
advances of the band stallions. She never
gave a bachelor a passing glance.*

This time, a black band stallion named Tucson bred her. When Electra tried to rejoin her band, Tucson herded her back. She broke away and headed to her mother with Tucson on her heels. Raven rushed in and intercepted the black, rearing and striking out at him with his front legs, backing him off. But when Tucson returned a second time, Raven only watched as the stallion galloped in and snaked Electra away. Raven seemed unwilling to invest more energy to keep his yearling daughter with the band.

Tucson chased her from one side of the huge meadow to the other with his ears back and his head held less than a foot from the ground. It's amazing how fast a stallion can run in this unnatural and uncomfortable-looking position, but Tucson made it look easy. Electra tried time after time to circle back to her band, but he cut her off again and again. Finally, the yearling gave in and Tucson pushed her into his band.

Tucson's grulla mare and three-year-old daughter lunged at Electra, trying to bite her. I'd seen mares react this way before, resentful of a new female in their established family. If they refused to accept Electra, there was little Tucson could do. He would be run ragged chasing her back simply to have his mares drive her away. Electra whinnied pathetically for Gray Bear, who answered her, but it was no use. Eventually Tucson would lose Electra, but she never returned to Raven's band nor did she ever give a bachelor a passing glance.

ELEVEN

The Storm

Another winter passed, and there was no sighting of Cloud. When the snows fell on the Arrowheads, burying the mountaintop in a soft blanket of white, where did he go? I found most of the horses foraging on the windswept ridges or down in the desert. His brother Diamond had shockingly stolen Raven's palomino mare and her filly daughter, and they grazed the winter away in the low country only a quarter of a mile from Raven. It's odd that the magnificent black stallion didn't challenge his impudent son, but I never saw him try to win back the mare.

I was confident Cloud was not down here. Days and weeks of searching over two winters never turned up a sighting of the white stallion. Hours of peering through my spotting scope at the open ridges midway up Sykes and Tillet Ridge produced a wonderful record of horse bands in winter but never a glimpse of Cloud. When I stopped to think about it, I had been able to follow this wandering stallion only from late May until October. Over half of his life remained a mystery to me. Unlike last winter, however, I was less worried, trying to believe that he would again appear with the melting of the snow and the greening of the high meadows. Yet, a nagging fear crept into my mind like water seeping through razor-thin cracks. The worry wouldn't really go away until I saw Cloud's beautiful white coat reflecting the sun from across the wide, flower-strewn meadows of the Arrowheads. "Until then, Cloud," I whispered as I left to go back home to Colorado.

Spring arrived with a fury. A terrific electrical storm pummeled the Arrowheads in June. Rain fell in stinging, wind-driven sheets, and lightning bolts repeatedly struck the mountaintop. A few days later, I slipped and slid in my four-wheeler up the rough old road to the first snow-rimmed bowl and stopped. Even from afar I could see a light buckskin mare, and knew I was looking at Raven's band; but there were no foals. This was a first. Then I saw the palomino mare and knew I had found Diamond's little band. Her light-colored filly from last year was at her side. I couldn't see Cloud, so I pressed forward through the mud to within a hundred yards of Penn's cabin.

Ravens circled overhead, which wasn't unusual, but this certainly was a large flock. When they lit above the snow-fed water hole, I stopped and got out. I walked up the rise to get a better view of the birds. The brisk west wind was blowing in my face, carrying with it a rancid odor.

The next morning dawned clear and calm. I went out looking for Cloud. Within an hour, I spotted him on the greening hilltop, sparring.

Through my binoculars, I saw the limb of a downed tree and a row of boulders. Strange, I didn't remember a tree out there or big rocks. Within a few minutes, I stood on a hill, where I had a better view of the area. Horses I had known for years lay dead below me. The Count, a black band stallion, lay on his side, one hind leg sticking grotesquely into the air like the limb of a dead tree. Nearby, two grulla mares lay dead on their sides. Next to one of the mares was a small dun foal, his body nestled close to his mother's side. All had surely been struck down by the lightning. Ravens had pecked out their eyes, but their bloated carcasses had proven too tough for the birds to open.

Shaken, I made my way back to the four-wheeler when more birds flew up from the other side of the road. My stomach flip-flopped as I went to investigate. *Oh, please, dear God, don't let it be Cloud*, I thought. Just past the stand of fir trees at the edge of the cliff where I had seen the young black bear two years before

Another winter passed and there was no sighting of Cloud. I found most of the horses foraging on the windswept ridges or down in the desert.

lay the body of the grulla band stallion, Challenger. He too had been struck down by lightning, collapsing at the edge of a melting snowdrift. I knelt down to examine his body. His throat and stomach had been torn open and eaten on. Tracks in the snow, like the footprints of a human, led from the stallion's body, across the snowfield, and down into a little tree-lined valley. *Poor Challenger*, I thought. Walking back to the four-wheeler, I felt a chill from the biting wind and pulled the collar up on my coat.

The next morning dawned clear and calm. I went out looking for Cloud. Within an hour, I spotted him on the greening hilltop, sparring with the black band stallion, Boomer. I breathed a sigh of relief at seeing him and moved closer. Four-year-old Cloud, dyed the color of Cheetos, no doubt from rolling in the red mud of the little intermittent water holes, looked like a horse from the *Wizard of Oz*. He touched noses with Boomer, then they both jerked their heads back and screamed in unison. Boomer wheeled around as if to kick, but Cloud countered before the older stallion could get his hind legs in the air. *Impressive*, I thought. Cloud was perfecting his fighting style. Both stallions parted amicably, and the ritualized duel was over. Cloud strode proudly across the rim of the hill, the snow-covered Beartooth Mountains towering in the background.

When Cloud looked over at me, I stopped and waved. How remarkable. Cloud was either impossible to find or incredibly easy to spot. "Hello boy," I whispered. "How have you been? And *where* have you been?" Muscles rippled under his pale orange coat. He was sleek, and his luxurious tail, dyed an even deeper orange than his body, touched the ground.

A five-year-old blue roan bachelor and a blue roan yearling walked over to greet him. *That's strange*, I thought, *a yearling should still be with his band*. Then I realized who the yearling was. "You're the Count's son, aren't you, fella?" When his band was struck down by lightning, he found a home with the bachelors, a year or so ahead of schedule. Cloud gently touched noses with the orphan, but the older bachelor quickly moved between them, claiming the young horse for himself. I'd seen older males adopt younger ones, treating them protectively as they would a mare. Ironically, the blue roan doing the adopting had himself been adopted as a yearling.

Cloud moved a short distance away and started grazing. I could study the many nicks and scabs on his coat. It was obvious he had been fighting. I didn't think too much about it until I learned that a BLM employee had watched Cloud fighting with Challenger on the day of the storm. They were fighting on the very spot where the grulla stallion was later killed. Cloud was lucky he wasn't lying dead atop the snowfield!

*Cloud had been fighting with
Challenger on the day of the
storm. They were fighting on
the very spot where the stallion
had been killed later that day.*

Day and night, day after day, week after week, it continued. Both Cloud and Mateo were losing weight under the strain of the chases and skirmishes.

TWELVE

Mateo

The next morning, Cloud moved into the teacup-shaped bowl. He was near a band of horses led by the stallion I had named Mateo years before. Mateo had always reminded me of a short, stocky dark-brown bear, so I named him *Mateo*, one of the words for "bear" in the Lakota Sioux language. When Cloud was released after the roundup, it was Mateo and his mare who were released with him. His band had grown since then, even though he had lost his blaze-faced mare to lightning the year before.

Mateo eyed Cloud suspiciously but continued to graze, so Cloud moved in a little closer, nonchalantly eating a few bites and taking a small step toward the band. When Mateo's mare urinated, Cloud lifted his head in the air, inhaled deeply, and raised his upper lip to expose his front teeth, a behavior known as *flehmen*. The stallion was filling his nasal passages with the scent of the mare. Mateo overmarked the spot where she had peed and then moved in and bred her as Cloud watched from a respectful distance.

The mating completed, Cloud whinnied, and Mateo pivoted to face the four-year-old stallion. Cloud took a step toward the band. Without a second's hesitation, Mateo charged—his head outstretched and his ears flattened. Cloud turned tail and ran. Around the huge bowl they sailed, the shorter, stockier stallion trying to bite the rear of the faster, longer-legged one. They tore through the broken trees and over hillsides littered with boulders. Suddenly, Cloud turned on Mateo, and they bit at each other furiously, rearing and then falling on their knees to protect vulnerable leg tendons from slashing teeth. Cloud bounced to his feet and took off again, the race continuing until both slowed and stopped. Mateo walked back to his band, breathing heavily, while Cloud watched with his sides heaving.

In time, the whole scenario repeated itself with Cloud nonchalantly nibbling a few blades of grass and moving ever so slowly nearer the band until he broke the invisible line that was Mateo's comfort zone. The bay ran at Cloud, who gave ground immediately, and

When Mateo's mare urinated, Cloud lifted his head in the air, inhaled deeply, and raised his upper lip to expose his front teeth, a behavior known as flehmen.

the chase was on again. On one such mad chase, Mateo reached out and grabbed a bit of Cloud's tail. I could see the long hair still attached but dragging on the ground.

Day and night, day after day, week after week, it continued. Both stallions were losing weight under the strain of the chases and skirmishes. Mateo's band seemed weary, too, for no sooner had they stopped to graze than Mateo herded them away in an effort to keep them from Cloud. And Cloud worked hard to keep any other stallion away from the horses in Mateo's band. If anyone was going to win them, it would be him.

Cloud entered his grunge phase that summer, constantly rolling in dirt and mud. His once pristine coat was filthy and scarred from fighting. He rolled in the muddiest parts of the water hole, then added extra layers by rolling in dust while his coat was still wet.

Perhaps he thought by becoming a dark horse he would look tougher. He was tougher, and he was short-tempered and aggressive even toward his closest bachelor allies. Any stallion who ventured close to Mateo's band was fair game.

I believed that it was Cloud's strategy to wear Mateo down, hoping the stocky bay would give up in time or let his guard down. It was a strategy that did not pan out for Cloud. At the close of another day of endless chases, I watched him trot across the skyline at sunset, his slender outline silhouetted against red and amber thunderheads. Then he appeared to trip, his head dropping to keep him from losing his balance. Cloud began limping badly on his left front leg. He stopped and looked at Mateo's band trailing away toward water, but this time he did not follow. After all his efforts, would an injury prevent him from winning a mare?

By morning, Cloud was out on an island of land I had named after him since it seemed a favorite place of his. He was rubbing on a low branch. When I got closer, I could see the welts that covered his back and sides and shoulders. First he rubbed his back on the limb, then his neck. Then he turned his butt to the trunk and rubbed. What had happened to him? Had he reacted badly to something he had eaten, or was he so stressed out that he had the horse equivalent of hives? In time he walked listlessly out to join the other bachelors. His limp was nearly undetectable at a walk, but I sensed he was hurting. He lay down at the feet of a black bachelor. It was his friend Zeppelin, a stunning bachelor who was just a year younger than Cloud. His unusual name was given him because he was such a dirigible-sized colt. Zep, as I called him, and Cloud had been friends ever since the black became a bachelor as a two-year-old. Cloud rolled flat and fell asleep, his head nearly touching Zep's hoof.

I sat down nearby and reflected. It is my belief that Cloud had been looking to replace the safety and security he had known in Raven's band by creating his own family. He had tried so hard, nearly killing himself in the process. What other four-year-old would have tried to wrest a band from a mature stallion in his prime? I watched his steady breathing, his ribs showing as he inhaled. His once pristine coat was a mass of scars, bumps, and open sores. But he would gain weight, and his sores and scars would heal over in time. I believed his leg would mend if he let it. What worried me most on this beautiful summer day was the inside of Cloud. Had his spirit been broken?

I watched Looking Glass and his band, and I shuddered to think of Cloud ever getting into a fight with this big dun band stallion.

THIRTEEN

Looking Glass

Just over the next hill from Cloud's bachelor band, another drama was unfolding. I watched excitedly from behind a stand of fir trees as a newborn black foal in Boomer's band struggled to stand. I envisioned capturing its first tentative steps on film. Time after time it would rise on its front legs, sitting on its haunches like a dog. Then, when it tried to position its back legs underneath its body, they collapsed, and the foal tumbled onto the grass.

Boomer's sorrel mare protected the foal from her curious two-year-old son. She drove him back when he tried to paw the little one. Boomer walked up and seemed to try to give the foal encouragement as he bowed his head low. I could almost hear him say, "Get up now, little one," as he towered over the tiny foal, softly touching its nose with his. But hour after hour went by. Try as it would, the foal just could not get its back legs to work. Most wild horse foals are up and nursing within an hour or two, and it had been four hours just since I had happened on the scene.

That's when another band came trotting into the meadow. It was Looking Glass's band. The big dun stallion jogged up behind his mares and stopped to glare at Boomer. The subordinate black stallion got the message, and he and his little band started to leave. The foal tried to get up and follow them but flopped back down. It was no use.

Most wild horse foals
are up and nursing
within an hour or two.

Looking Glass's lead mare noticed the dark shape in the grass and hesitantly went to investigate. When she was within a few feet of the foal, she stretched out her neck and sniffed. Then she took another step and slowly touched the foal, who immediately responded by trying to stand. But it toppled over in a heap. Then Looking Glass approached, and the mare backed off. The dun was careful, too, sniffing from a few feet away before tentatively putting his nose on the foal's back and sniffing again. That's when the unexpected happened.

The stallion took hold of the foal's back with his teeth and lifted it, violently and repeatedly shaking it and slamming it to the ground. The mares screamed and dashed in circles around the stallion, trying to stop his attack, but he paid no attention to them. Looking Glass gave the foal one last deadly shake, and then, with his ears laid flat, he drove his mares away.

Boomer charged in, but it was too late. He retreated to his mare and son, who waited for him on the hill. Then, for some inexplicable reason, Looking Glass stopped and walked some distance back to the lifeless body of the foal. Did he want to check to make sure it was dead? Slowly and just as tentatively as the first time, he sniffed the dead body and walked away.

I could hardly believe what I had seen. It was with some caution that I emerged from the little grove of firs. I walked to the foal and knelt down. She was a little filly. I had read about stallions taking over a band and acting aggressive to stud foals but not to fillies. Why her, then? I wondered if he killed the foal because she didn't get out of his way, which would have been proper foal etiquette. Did he kill her because he feared her? Did he kill her because she was sick? Did he know she wasn't his and was eliminating the competition for his own foals? A million questions flooded my head as I stroked her dark, silky baby coat and touched the tiny upright mane. Her body lay peacefully among the deep pink wild flowers. Shooting stars are some of my favorite flowers, and they wreathed her perfectly formed head. I could rationalize that Looking Glass did her a favor, saving her from a lingering death, for she was not destined to dance atop the Arrowheads with the other foals. Still, there was no avoiding the violence of this haunting and disturbing act.

Slowly, the sounds around me started to filter back in as my mind cleared. I heard the familiar rat-a-tat of a woodpecker hammering a hollow limb, the sound echoing across the valley. Juncos chirped and flitted in the stand of firs behind me, and chickadees called a dee-dee-dee from the forest. A mountain bluebird hovered low then landed to capture a grasshopper. Life went on as if nothing had happened, but I would never forget what I had seen. I knew for sure that I would forever view this stallion and all horses differently. They are like people. Some are gentle, others violent, and a few are truly dangerous. I shuddered to think of Cloud ever getting into a fight with this big dun band stallion.

I could hardly believe what I had seen. It was with some caution that I emerged from the little grove of firs. I walked to the foal and knelt down.

Many healthy, vigorous foals were missing. One missing foal was the little black with the big star and snip who I called Two Moons.

FOURTEEN

Death Stalks the Mountaintop

I crawled on my hands and knees up an open hillside and then slid on my stomach behind a small stand of trees. Their trunks are twisted from the near-continuous pounding they take on the edge of this windy cliff. Carefully, I pulled aside a low branch and watched as a beautiful cinnamon bear a quarter mile off ambled across the open slope separated from me by a deep but narrow valley. As he sauntered, he scattered a flock of ravens, whose protesting caws were swallowed up in the stiff wind. The bear stopped and sat on his haunches next to the body of a bay mare. Her blaze face and white stockings identified her to me as the lead mare in Sandman's band. She had died giving birth, and by the time I arrived on the mountain, the bear had feasted repeatedly on her misfortune. The ravens landed cautiously, hoping to share in the leftovers. The bear looked up and sniffed the air. I laid flat on the ground, hoping that the changing wind would pass over my scent without telegraphing my presence. But I had been detected. He rose on all fours and looked around, then left unhurriedly, melting into the limber pines on the wooded slope.

The next day, I hid behind a pile of rocks, watching as the same bear feasted on one of the lightning-struck horses. His gorgeous deep cinnamon coat was blowing in the early morning breeze. And in the late afternoon, I sneaked up in the rocks overlooking Challenger's body. The once beautiful grulla stallion had been dragged from the top of the snowdrift all the way down into the little valley. A young black bear crawled inside his chest cavity to pull out the rotting flesh. A marmot above him peeked out of his rocky den to watch and then ducked back in his hole.

The bear was black as night with a mealy tan nose, and he was hungry. He used his front paw to drag the huge carcass closer to the trees, and then he gnawed on the skull and looked up to sniff. I was less than 100 feet away and 20 or 30 feet above him. I was sure he could smell me, but his hunger overcame his normal caution. I could see he had a crippled front leg and needed to take advantage of this rare opportunity, regardless of the risks. What had happened to him? Bear hunters were common in the spring and fall. Perhaps he had been shot. I hoped that Challenger's death might help to sustain

How many horses would die this summer? I started to notice that foals were missing in almost every band.

him until he could recover, if recovery was possible. His claws were useable for holding onto and dragging the carcass, but the leg itself seemed paralyzed.

How many horses would die this summer? Death seemed to stalk the mountaintop. I started to notice missing foals in almost every band. One tiny *grulla* had been born premature and I imagined she had died. Perhaps coyotes had dragged off her emaciated carcass. But many other healthy, vigorous foals were missing. There was the little black with the big star and snip who I called Two Moons and a dun foal with a huge star who I called Cheyenne. There was a little dark brown colt I named York for the black sergeant in the Lewis and Clark Expedition and a colt in Plenty Coups's band who was so bold he ran with the bachelors when they thundered through. Both of Raven's foals had disappeared in the spring along with others. I believed a mountain lion or perhaps several mountain lions had developed an addiction for tender wild horse babies.

In August, I returned to look for Cloud only to find that he and the other bachelors had disappeared from the central part of the range. So I started to search in the higher meadows, where many of the horses graze in late summer. That's where I found a hunk of Cloud's once beautiful tail pulled loose in a running battle with Mateo. I wound it up and put it carefully in a compartment of my backpack, knowing how remarkable it was that I had found it or had been led to it. It was special to have this tangible part of a stallion who so captivated me.

I followed tracks that converged into a horse highway through the forest, leading from one sheltered meadow to another. I was heading toward Lost Water Canyon, a maze of dramatic canyons created when the ocean floor rose up, cracked, and shifted, splintering into crevasses cut deeper by wind and water with each passing millennia. The trail climbed through dense trees and onto an open meadow. This place was familiar to me only by a name on the topographical map and the stories of horse deaths here in the winter of 1977. It was Tony's Island, a finger of land with a year-round spring, where many older horses and all the foals died in an icy winter storm.

A little dark-brown colt I named York was
a foal who fell prey to a mountain lion.

Even the powerful legs of the adults failed to break through the thick layer of ice, and the horses starved to death.

I followed an old two-track road only visible on the rocky parts of the trail. Ahead were what looked like bones lying among the late-blooming flowers. They were bones—small, unbleached ones. This was a fresh site. Close by, a piece of skin with dun-colored hair firmly attached lay twisted in the grass. I realized I was looking at the remains of the foal we called Cheyenne, the one with the huge star. His skull and most of his backbone were missing. Little legs lay scattered around in the field. In another half mile, I found his band grazing on the side of a canyon, and I sat down nearby to watch them. Like many of the bands that year, there were no foals left, but one of the mares looked like she could give birth any day. Most foals had been born months ago in late May and early June and had the chance to grow strong before winter set in. This one was going to get a late start.

Far down the ridge, shapes moved between the dark trunks of Douglas firs. Horses. Six, including Cloud, walked out and leisurely trailed through a field of blue-green sage, passing under a dead fir where a family of kestrels had lit only to launch into the clear blue sky with the passing of the stallions. The little falcons with tapered wings dove into the sage, and one of them plucked an unsuspecting grasshopper out of the dirt. As the horses moved upward, a sage grouse burst from cover and flew on a low trajectory into another patch of sage. This was the one and only time I ever saw this largest member of the grouse family on the Arrowheads. But I imagined there were more.

Cloud and the bachelors trailed to the spring-fed water hole, a reliable source of water even in late summer, when the snow-fed holes had dried up. The isolation here on Tony Island made a perfect hideaway. I watched as the other bachelors pawed the water and played, while Cloud stood listless. When he trailed off with them, I couldn't detect any lameness but felt he was not himself. He had a bump on his nose, perhaps from fighting, and his once beautiful tail was scraggly. He hadn't gained back as much weight as I thought he might have. But these outward signs were not as troubling to me as his attitude. Had he lost his will to become a band stallion?

The bachelors were still hanging out on Tony's Island, even though most of the family bands had migrated to lower elevations.

FIFTEEN

Lost Water Canyon

W inter came early that year. By September, the snow had begun to fly, and the wind howled. The bachelors were still hanging out on Tony's Island, even though all but one family band had migrated down the mountain. It was the band with the mare who had foaled in August, but she had no baby. Another mountain lion kill? I imagined the big cats were particularly active out here.

Cloud had picked up weight. Whether it was enough to carry him through winter, I wasn't sure. I began to suspect that he and at least some of the bachelors would stay out here, braving the steep canyons and deep snows.

Then, in November, I spoke with a deer hunter who said that several years before he had seen a beautiful white horse running on a road in the area of the Big Ice Cave, which is far outside the horse range. It had no doubt been Cloud. This was the reason I could never find him in winter. He had spent perhaps every year as a bachelor in the seclusion of Lost Water Canyon. If I were to track him in winter, this is where I would need to come.

In January, I launched my most ambitious search for Cloud, believing I had located at least the area in which to look. The drifts were 6 feet deep in places, and I waded through them in my snowshoes. It was slow going, but I'd seen tracks and believed there were horses in an area of Lost Water Canyon called Commissary Ridge. I noticed deer tracks inside the horse tracks, the delicate cloven hooves following in the large round holes made by the solid-hoofed horses. The horses help to open pathways in deep snow for the deer and break holes in the ice, allowing smaller, weaker animals to drink.

*In January, I launched my most
ambitious search for Cloud. The
drifts were 6 feet deep in places.*

My heart leapt as I caught a distant view of wild horses. All were dark, but Cloud could be in the trees behind them. I tried to walk faster, but each step was difficult, and I fell several times. Have you ever tried to get up while wallowing in 6 feet of snow with your snowshoes buried underneath you? It isn't easy, and the struggling—and the cold—sapped my energy. But I focused on getting close enough to the horses to identify them. There weren't any foals, not that I could see. That was a good sign, for foals would mean a family band for sure.

The closer I got, however, the more I realized who they were. It was a band led by the black stallion Opposite, Trace's father. He had a young stallion and two mares, but no foals who had survived in this disastrous year. Probably a mountain lion had claimed them as they had so many others. I stopped, sat back in the snow with my legs outstretched, and grabbed my binoculars from my backpack. When I focused in, I was amazed to see how fat they were. Out here they dug for every bite of food, but they were plump.

An excited yipping call sliced the silence. Perhaps the coyote was celebrating a catch.

Opposite's bay lead mare eyed me suspiciously and then continued to forage. I doubt these horses saw many people, especially in the dead of winter. Clouds of steam poured out of their mouths and evaporated into the chill, dry air. They pawed holes in the snow and dipped their heads in for a bite of grass. It might be difficult to get to, but it's nutritious. With virtually no competition, there was a lot to eat.

The wind died down, and I could hear the distant call of a raven. I sat daydreaming, imagining how it must have been a few hundred years ago when there were places like this all across North America, places where the law of nature ruled, and life moved to the rhythms of the earth. An excited yipping call sliced the silence. Perhaps the coyote was celebrating a catch. I noticed a golden eagle soaring low over the treetops. How I wished I could grab onto her wide wings so she could carry me low over the snowy canopy and down deep into the canyons. I would be sure to find Cloud then. "How about a lift?" I whispered. The big bird continued down the rim of a canyon wall and disappeared.

Cloud had picked up weight.
Whether it was enough to
carry him through winter,
I wasn't sure.

Cloud and Plenty Coups battled toe to toe for a few seconds until both noticed that Conquistador had started to drive Plenty Coups's mares away.

SIXTEEN

The Battle

By early May, I still had not found Cloud. I took heart, though, when my friend Trish Kerby saw him from an airplane while flying in the Big Ice Cave area of the Arrowheads. In a clearing surrounded by dense forest and isolated on three sides by steep cliffs, she saw what looked like a white log. When the log moved, she circled to take a closer look. It was Cloud. He was with a solid black horse. I imagined it was his friend Zeppelin. Before Trish could see much more, Cloud melted into the trees. To my knowledge, she has been the only person to see him before he decided to be seen. The year before, bear hunters swore they saw a white horse racing through the deep timber on upper Sykes Ridge, but I always took that bit of information with a grain of salt.

I returned to the Arrowheads in late May, and on my way up Tillet Ridge Road, as I rounded a curve in the forest, a small black bear darted across the old two-track road and into the timber. I figured it was a young bear or perhaps a female. Colorado had banned spring bear hunting, but not Montana. "Hurry away, little bear," I whispered. Much as I wanted to watch him forage and do his bear things, I wanted more for him to make himself invisible, at least until the hunters left the forest. I'd seen a number of bears in the Arrowheads, but every new sighting was a thrill.

In the open limber pine forest near the top of the mountain, I stopped to watch several mule deer does lying in a sunny spot between trees. A slight movement well behind them grabbed my attention. I skirted the deer and made my way to a low rise and ducked down between two pines, careful to stay downwind. Through my binoculars, I could see three tiny balls of fur at the opening of a den. Coyote pups! I had looked for a den for years but had never found one.

The pups, probably six weeks old or so, looked toward the trees where I hid, but the wind was still blowing in my face, so I felt sure they couldn't smell me. I waited, and in time they lost interest in something they couldn't see or smell and started playing. They rolled and tumbled end over end and leapt over the low clumps of sage near the den. One pup ventured a little farther, and I saw him tip his head one way and then another while

By early May, I still had not found Cloud. On Sykes Ridge, I found a mare high above the Bighorn Canyon.

he stared at the ground and then leapt in the air, pouncing on what must have been a grasshopper. He munched the insect down and began to stalk again. Suddenly, all three sat bolt upright and stared back into the forest. I watched an adult coyote trot out of the trees. When she broke into a lope, something clicked in my memory bank, for she held one leg in the air when she ran. I knew this animal! I had seen her two years ago out near Tony's Island. It was the same crippled adult; I was sure of it.

She trotted toward the pups, who raced to meet her, smothering their mother in wet kisses. The pups solicited a meal by grabbing her muzzle and licking her face. She obliged by repeatedly regurgitating voles. The first chubby rodent was snatched up by the alpha pup, then two more were regurgitated for the lesser ranking pups. How incredibly excited I was to see this behavior. If the mother coyote had any inkling I was watching, she would never have regurgitated the meal but would have led the pups away into the forest. It's entirely possible she would have abandoned the den site for another.

About that time, wild horses trotted over the hill and through the trees. It was Mateo and his band, which included Cloud's sister, Electra, the beautiful red roan with the lightning bolt on her face. Mercifully, she had not foaled as a two-year-old—at least I never saw a foal. But this year as a three-year-old, she had a handsome blue roan colt, petite like his mother. They passed by the coyotes, who sat watching them intently. I watched the horses trot off with Mateo pushing them along, his head low and his ears laid back. When I looked back to the coyote den, the mother had slipped away. That's when I sneaked off, too, before I was spotted.

I had barely stashed my gear in Penn's cabin before all hell broke loose in the meadows nearby. I trotted up the hill and looked down into the greening field of grass to see at least fifty horses in close proximity to each other. A quarter mile away from the big group was Cloud. He was sparring with the dun bachelor Conquistador. Broken, fast-moving clouds darkened the meadows except for a little patch of sunlight

The coyote pups looked toward the trees where I hid, but the wind was still blowing in my face, so I felt sure they couldn't smell me.

that had fallen on the rearing white stallion. On this huge mountain landscape, Cloud was the old Cloud again, bold and ready to claim center stage.

Racing for my camera gear, I set up in a spot where I could film the action. It was chaotic, with band stallions trying to steal each other's mares. The blue roan stallion Plenty Coups had made off with one of the dun stallion Prince's, mares, and Prince was charging after Plenty Coups to get her back. Boomer, his mare, and his new black foal were just traveling through and had to gallop away to avoid getting caught up in the conflict. I could see Diamond, the palomino, her yearling, and their new foals on the hillside, watching.

Then, out of the corner of my eye, I saw Cloud charging up from well down in the valley, whinnying as he ran. There wasn't a trace of any lameness. Had he sensed an opening? Plenty Coups was trying to recover his new mare from Prince and had left his band unguarded. Cloud began running beside a blue roan mare and her filly foal, trying to haze them away from the band, but the mare was not about to leave her comrades.

*Plenty Coups had made off
with one of Prince's mares,
and Prince was charging after
Plenty Coups to get her back.
Here, Prince is running with
his band.*

She broke into a dead run with her foal running beside her as if she had been attached to her mother with Velcro. Plenty Coups spun around when he noticed Cloud. Giving up on the idea of theft, Plenty Coups had to concentrate on keeping his family together.

Plenty Coups cut Cloud away from the band. The two battled toe to toe for a few seconds until both noticed that Conquistador had started to drive Plenty Coups's mares away. Cloud couldn't let Conquistador make off with the band, and Plenty Coups was equally determined to run them both off. So here was Cloud, chasing Conquistador off, while Plenty Coups bore down on Cloud. As they raced into a stand of trees, Plenty Coups stretched out his neck, and, with bared teeth, he caught hold of Cloud, ripping a hole in his rear. Blood spurted from the wound, but if it hurt Cloud, he didn't let on. He was after Conquistador, determined to teach the bigger horse a lesson.

While Plenty Coups returned to get his band back together, Cloud caught Conquistador in the open field. They both reared up and pawed the air, screaming. They lashed out with lightning-fast strikes of their front feet, glancing blows that didn't seem to deter the other. They spun and kicked at each other with their hind legs, and then Cloud pivoted and ran back toward Plenty Coups and his band. Conquistador stopped and watched. Had Cloud's warning dissuaded the older stallion, or was Conquistador just biding his time?

Cloud raced toward Plenty Coups, and the blue roan trotted out to face the white stallion. But when they were within a few yards of each other, Cloud suddenly veered to the right, and Plenty Coups gave chase. Again, it seemed to be Cloud's strategy to make the band stallion chase him rather than meet the blue roan stallion in head-to-head combat. Plenty Coups seemed willing to oblige. With Cloud in front, Plenty Coups charged after him, the two stallions in a dead run across the meadows. Then, Plenty Coups seemed to stumble. His left front leg gave out on him, and he skipped to a stop. Blood ran down his leg.

Then, out of the corner of my eye, I saw
Cloud charging up from well down in
the valley, whinnying as he ran.

Plenty Coups's leg ballooned up, and he licked the oozing blood from the open hole around his knee as Cloud continued to canter away. Looking over his shoulder at his injured rival, Cloud slowed down and stood watching as Plenty Coups licked his wound. Was this an old injury suddenly reopened? Was it an injury suffered in a duel with Prince that morning, or had Cloud caught him with a hoof in their brief skirmish? I will never be sure. Cloud wasn't exactly the picture of health either. At some point in all the fighting, he had lost the tip of his right ear. Dried blood encrusted it as well as the hole in his hip. But he was sound. I detected no lameness during all his running.

The wind had picked up by afternoon, blowing in the fog. Cloud dogged Plenty Coups and his band, keeping all other stallions, including Conquistador, from the group. The blue roan stallion was not about to give up his family. When Cloud baited

him into long runs, Plenty Coups followed, running bravely on three legs. It was a replay of Cloud versus Mateo, but this time Cloud had a wounded adversary.

In the fog, I saw a dun stallion emerge. It was Looking Glass. Cloud saw him, too, and trotted confidently toward the much larger horse. Both deposited on a stud pile, and Cloud struck out at the stallion with both of his front legs, stomping them down nearly together. I'd seen Cloud do this more than once. It was becoming his unique greeting dance that seemed to say, "Back off before somebody gets hurt." Looking Glass shook his dark mane in irritation. I waited for him to attack, but he did the unexpected: he trotted off, still shaking his head. *Thank goodness*, I thought. Ever since seeing Looking Glass kill the foal, I had dreaded an altercation between him and Cloud.

The fog thickened, and I lost Cloud and Plenty Coups as they once again took up the chase. But I could still hear their eerie screams, which seemed so much clearer in the fog than on a sunny day. Is my hearing more acute when I can't rely on my sight, or does the damp fog somehow amplify the calls? Every once in a while the fog would clear a little, and I would be able to see Cloud before he was swallowed up again.

The storm lasted for days. I retreated to huddle around the little stove in Penn's cabin but jumped up to look out the open door when I heard horses trotting by. Sometimes I could make them out, passing like ghosts in the mist. Time was running out for me. My wood supply was dwindling and so was my food and water. I had to leave the mountaintop without knowing what had happened to Cloud and Plenty Coups.

Cloud dogged Plenty Coups and his band, keeping all other stallions, including Conquistador, from the group.

In the distance, we saw a
few bands of horses, and
I knew Trace was curious.

SEVENTEEN

The Journey

In late August, I made good on a promise to Trace, and together we traveled back to his home to look for Cloud. It was a cool, windy morning when we rode out on a well-used wild horse trail near Tony's Island. I knew it was familiar to Trace, for I had seen him with his mother and Flash at a water hole near here. He walked out so briskly that I wondered how he kept from breaking into a trot. His ears were forward and he looked from side to side. In the distance, we saw a few bands of horses, and I knew he was curious. We traveled along the edge of the little spring-fed lake, and a group of bachelors came out of the woods to eye us curiously. It was Plenty Coups, his bachelor son, and a bay. Plenty Coups's leg was still badly swollen, and it was obvious he had lost his mares.

We walked to the water's edge, and Trace calmly got a drink while I kept an eye on the bachelors. I didn't want them to think it was time for some stallion play. I needn't have worried, for they kept a cautious distance. Then, all of the sudden, Trace plunged belly-deep into the lake and started pawing the water into white, frothy waves. Water was flying everywhere, and all I could do was laugh—that is, until I felt his legs buckle. He's going to roll in the water! He doesn't care that he has a passenger on his back—a passenger who is not one bit interested in a swim. As quickly as I could, I got a tighter hold on the reins and turned him around. Clucking, I nudged him forward. Oh so reluctantly, he waded out and up on the bank. I jumped off, hoping to avoid a repeat performance. Clark's nutcrackers that were perched in the trees above us cawed in a raspy chorus. Somehow, it sounded a lot like laughter.

I led Trace toward the center of the horse-range meadows. I could see Diamond and the palomino, their roan yearling, and their foal. Not too far away, beautiful Raven and his mares and foals grazed. He had picked up two more mares and had three foals in his band. They were foraging on grass that was tinder dry. Little rain had fallen that summer, and forest fires had eaten up millions of acres in the West. Even near the horse range, a small fire had been sparked by dry lightning but had been put out by alert firefighters.

In late August, I made good on a promise to my horse Trace, and together we traveled back to his home to look for Cloud.

Trace and I walked through trails in the firs. For a second, I thought I saw the flash of a light-colored horse running behind dense trees, but I wasn't sure. We startled a little flock of blue grouse, who burst up and landed in low branches. A doe leapt up and ran from her shady sleeping spot. Marmots barked a warning from a nearby cliff, and a red squirrel scolded from a tall Douglas fir. A cottontail nibbled on dry tufts of grass and hopped off into the forest when we passed.

Trace lifted his head and turned. I stopped and listened. Horses rely on movement and sound to detect trouble. That's why they can be spooky to ride on a windy day when the leaves are blowing and the noises are so confusing. I paid close attention when Trace heard something, or when he saw movement. We both stood very still and watched and listened. There it was again: a movement and a flash of something behind the trees in front of us. I know Trace saw it, too. Was it a light horse?

We startled a little flock of blue grouse, who burst up and landed in low branches.

I mounted and rode in a wide circle. I didn't want to frighten away whatever was back there. As we broke into the clear, I saw Cloud. "Hello, boy," I whispered. He looked up, and I waved. Cloud looked at the familiar gesture but the unfamiliar sight of that two-legged atop a four-legged. He snorted. Both Trace and I were motionless. I could sense Cloud was weighing whether to run or stand his ground. "It's OK, Cloud," I whispered more to myself than to him.

Cloud calmed down and started to graze. I breathed easier and took time to study the beautiful stallion before me. His cuts were less conspicuous. Hair was growing over his nipped-off ear tip. Most of all, though, I was struck at how fat he looked, fatter than I had ever seen him. That's when I saw a grulla mare, followed by her red dun son, walk out of the trees behind him. When they passed Cloud, he turned to follow. I knew I was looking at a family, Cloud's family.

I recognized the mare. Ironically, she was not from Plenty Coups's band but from King's. She had been with the bay stallion for nearly five years. Later, I learned from Trish Kerby that Cloud did not win the mare from King in a furious clash of teeth and hooves, but in a moment of stillness. She had given birth to a sickly foal. Instead of rejoining her band, she stayed with her newborn. Cloud found her and stood quietly by her side in the shade of a tree. When the foal died, the mare, her yearling, and Cloud stayed together.

As the threesome made their way to the water hole, I followed and watched from far away. They drank and moved on, not stopping to play. They grazed together, and Cloud and the yearling groomed each other. Clearly the yearling liked his young stepfather. I wasn't so sure about the mare. She was older and no doubt set in her ways. When Cloud tried to snake her, she ignored him. I thought to myself, *No more remote canyons and deep snows for you, Cloud. Now you may have to settle down to a life below the snow line. Maybe now I'll be able to find you in winter.*

The mare and yearling trotted ahead onto a wide plain. The Bighorn Basin stretched out far below them, and the distant Absarokee Mountains of Yellowstone gleamed in the distance. Cloud had fallen well behind his mare and ran to catch up, kicking up his heels like a lively colt. It seemed only an instant had passed since I worried that

the fragile white newborn might not live, and my fears were erased when I saw him dance confidently to the water hole for the first time. I remember how he ran rings around the clusters of firs and endlessly pestered his sisters. Most of all, I remember one evening at sunset. The sky was crimson and I sat quietly on a hilltop some distance away from Raven and his band. Cloud came over to me and touched my hair, his warm breath grazing my cheek. Then he walked away.

Cloud, the mare, and the yearling had stopped and were grazing together peacefully. I felt happy for Cloud, knowing he had won his struggle to start his own family. "Stay safe," I whispered. As I rode away, I kept looking back until I couldn't see Cloud anymore. I rode Trace out of the Arrowheads, down the long horse trail where generations of his ancestors had walked. We left the big meadows and deep canyons behind as we traveled the forested path down the mountain.

The seasons will pass and another spring will bring a new crop of wild horse babies. And maybe, just maybe, a Cloud colt will prance across the Arrowheads, as precocious and proud as his remarkable father—and, I hope, forever free.

I knew I was looking at a family, Cloud's family.

"Stay safe," I whispered. I felt happy
for Cloud, knowing he had won his
struggle to start his own family.

Epilogue

Remembering a Legend

In the years that followed, I continued to chronicle Cloud's exciting life in the Arrowheads. His adventures as a young band stallion and as a powerful adult are detailed in this book's sequels *Cloud: The Wild Stallion Returns* and *Cloud: Challenge of the Stallion*. The story of Cloud's final seven years has yet to be written, and, in many ways, they were the most dramatic of his life.

Cloud commanded the largest band on the mountain when he acquired his mare, Feldspar. This would prove to be a remarkable pairing. Three stunning Cloud-and-Feldspar offspring live free on the Pryor Mountains: Mato Ska, a beautiful blaze-faced blue roan colt; Mato Ska's little sister, Encore, who is a Cloud look-alike; and the pale buckskin colt Pride, a dead ringer in color to his grandmother, who is pictured on page 16 of this book.

Cloud was injured in a vicious fight in 2014 when he was nineteen years old. He temporarily lost Feldspar and his younger mare, Innocentes, and he permanently lost two-year-old Mato Ska as well as yearling Encore, who was stolen by a band of bachelor stallions the day after her first birthday. Cloud was able to win the mares back only to be injured again in early 2015, losing Innocentes and a pregnant Feldspar. The day after Cloud turned twenty, he made a gallant, unsuccessful try to win back Feldspar and his newborn son, Pride, who never knew Cloud as his father.

Cloud disappeared going into the winter of 2015. I saw him in March and May of 2016, but when I searched for him in the areas where I clearly saw him, I could not find him. In one inexplicable case, I found no horses at all. Cloud's body has never been found—appropriate for a legend.

Cloud's spirit is everywhere on the Pryors. His mother, sons and daughters, granddaughters and grandsons, nephews and nieces, and cousins carry on. I dedicate this beautifully revised edition of *Cloud, Wild Stallion of the Rockies* to my friend and inspiration, Cloud.

Five-day-old Pride and his mother, Feldspar.

The Cloud Foundation

Dedicated to the preservation of wild horses and burros on our public lands in the American West.

In 1995, Emmy-winning filmmaker Ginger Kathrens filmed a nearly white newborn foal in a remote and rugged corner of the Rocky Mountains. The unusual wild foal quickly won her heart and became the focus of her camera's eye.

Ginger has captured Cloud's life on film, first in *Cloud: Wild Stallion of Rockies,* voted the most popular program in the history of the acclaimed Nature series on PBS, which has been produced since 1982. This book, a companion to that acclaimed film, won the Colorado Book Awards when it was first published in 2001. Two more films and books followed, focusing on Cloud's life as a powerful band stallion and father: *Cloud's Legacy: The Wild Stallion Returns* and *Cloud: Challenge of Stallions.*

In 2005, fearing that Cloud and his family might be rounded up and removed from their spectacular home, a fate suffered by thousands of wild horses in the West, Ginger created The Cloud Foundation. Since that time, the foundation has been in the forefront of fighting for mustang and burro freedom. Ginger is a national spokesperson on the topic of Cloud, wild horse behavior, and innovative ways to manage mustang and burro herds without removing them from their homes on the range.

Join the movement to protect and preserve these national treasures. Visit The Cloud Foundation at www.thecloudfoundation.org. Follow the foundation on Facebook at "Cloud the Stallion." Volunteer to save the remaining wild herds. Shop at the Cloud Store, where you can find the DVD set containing all three Cloud programs and many beautiful gifts. Donate to protect and defend mustangs and burros still living in precious freedom. Adopt a mustang or burro and give the animal a new life—with you!

(The Cloud Foundation is a Colorado 501(c)3, and all donations are tax deductible.)

Selected Bibliography

Ainslie, Tom, and Bonnie Ledbetter. *The Body Language of Horses.* New York: William Morrow and Company, Inc., 1980.

Berger, Joel. *Wild Horses of the Great Basin: Social Competition and Population Size.* Chicago: The University of Chicago Press, 1986.

Dobie, J. Frank. *The Mustang.* New York: Bramhall House, 1952.

Farley, Terri. *Wild Hearts: Mustangs and the Young People Trying to Save Them.* Boston: Houghton Mifflin Harcourt, 2015.

Kania, Alan. *Wild Horse Annie: Velma Johnston and Her Fight to Save the Mustang.* Reno, NV: University of Nevada Press, 2012.

Kathrens, Ginger. *Cloud's Legacy: The Wild Stallion Returns.* Irvine, California: Bow Tie Press, 2002.

Kathrens, Ginger. *Cloud: Challenge of the Stallions.* Altona, Manitoba, Canada: Friesens Publishing, 2010.

Kirkpatrick, Jay F. *Into the Wind: Wild Horses of North America.* Minocqua, WI: NorthWord Press, 1994.

MacFadden, Bruce J. *Fossil Horses: Systematics, Paleobiology, and Evolution of the Family Equidae.* New York: Cambridge University Press, 1992.

Ryden, Hope. *America's Last Wild Horses.* New York: The Lyons Press, 1999.

Scanlon, Lawrence. *Wild About Horses: Our Timeless Passion for the Horse.* New York: Harper Collins, 1998.

Sponenberg, D. Phillip. *Equine Color Genetics.* Hoboken, NJ: Wiley Blackwell Publishing, 2009.

Stillman, Deanne. *Mustang: The Saga of the Wild Horse in the American West.* Boston: Mariner Books/Houghton Mifflin Harcourt, 2009.

Walker, Carol J. *Wild Hoofbeats: America's Vanishing Wild Horses.* Colorado: Longmont, CO: Painted Hills Publishing, 2008.

Index

Note: Page numbers in **bold** typeface indicate a photograph.

About the Author

Ginger Kathrens is an Emmy-winning wildlife filmmaker. She has filmed all over the world for the Discovery Channel, Animal Planet, NATURE, the BBC, PBS, and National Geographic, and she worked on more than twenty segments of the PBS series *Wild America* from 1987 to 1996, including the two-part program *Year of the Mustang*, which introduced her to the Pryor Mountains and Raven's band in early 1994. Since that time, Ginger has spent thousands of hours observing and filming wild horses not only on Cloud's home range but also all over the western United States as well as on Cumberland and Corolla Islands off the East Coast.

In 2005, Ginger founded The Cloud Foundation, a Colorado 501(c)3, to try to protect Cloud's Pryor Mountain herd and all herds in the West from the massive roundups she was witnessing. In a heartbeat, the wild horses she so admired were losing what they held most dear: their freedom and their families. Kathrens is executive director of the foundation and is a frequent speaker about her decades-long adventure with Cloud and his family and the continuing efforts of The Cloud Foundation to prevent the extinction of these inspiring animals.

Ginger lives on her ranch at the base of the Sangre de Cristo Mountains in southern Colorado that her Irish Terrier, Quinn, and her mustangs, Flint, Sky, Trace, Sax, BJ, and Swasey, share with the abundant wildlife of the Rockies.